THE BONES
Flash Cards

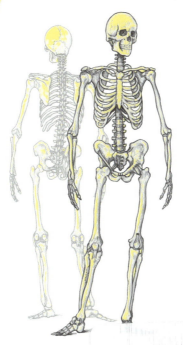

158 cards
Terminology
Definitions of Movemen[t]

D0145921

TABLE OF CONTENTS

THE SKELETAL SYSTEM

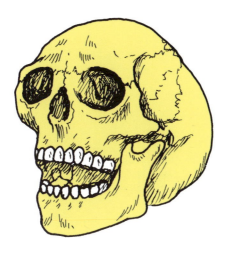

2

The Skull

External Skull

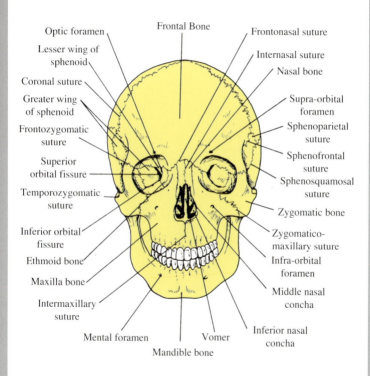

Optic foramen

Lesser wing of sphenoid

Coronal suture

Greater wing of sphenoid

Frontozygomatic suture

Superior orbital fissure

Temporozygomatic suture

Inferior orbital fissure

Ethmoid bone

Maxilla bone

Intermaxillary suture

Frontal Bone

Frontonasal suture

Internasal suture

Nasal bone

Supra-orbital foramen

Sphenoparietal suture

Sphenofrontal suture

Sphenosquamosal suture

Zygomatic bone

Zygomatico-maxillary suture

Infra-orbital foramen

Middle nasal concha

Inferior nasal concha

Mental foramen

Vomer

Mandible bone

View: Anterior

3

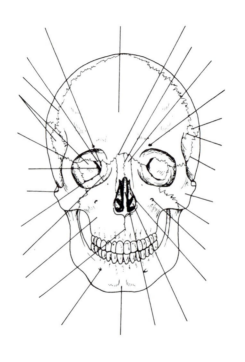

Orbital Cavity

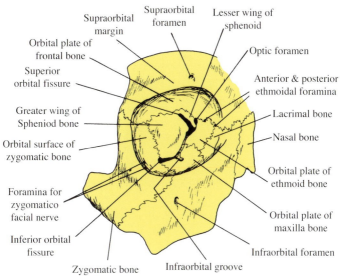

Supraorbital margin

Supraorbital foramen

Lesser wing of sphenoid

Orbital plate of frontal bone

Optic foramen

Superior orbital fissure

Anterior & posterior ethmoidal foramina

Greater wing of Sphenoid bone

Lacrimal bone

Nasal bone

Orbital surface of zygomatic bone

Orbital plate of ethmoid bone

Foramina for zygomatico facial nerve

Orbital plate of maxilla bone

Inferior orbital fissure

Infraorbital foramen

Zygomatic bone

Infraorbital groove

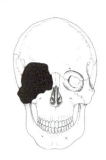

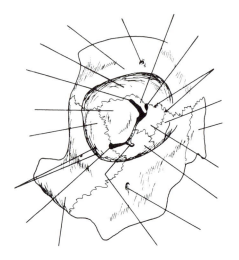

External Skull

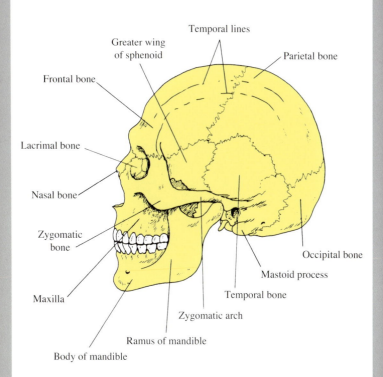

Temporal lines

Greater wing of sphenoid

Parietal bone

Frontal bone

Lacrimal bone

Nasal bone

Zygomatic bone

Maxilla

Occipital bone

Mastoid process

Temporal bone

Zygomatic arch

Ramus of mandible

Body of mandible

View: *Left lateral*

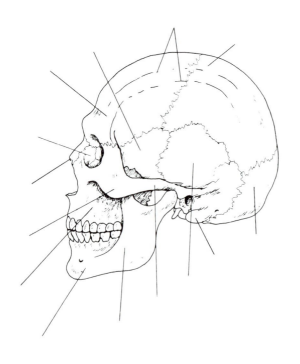

External Skull

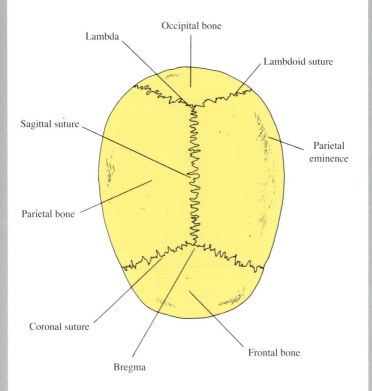

Occipital bone

Lambda

Lambdoid suture

Sagittal suture

Parietal eminence

Parietal bone

Coronal suture

Frontal bone

Bregma

View: Superior

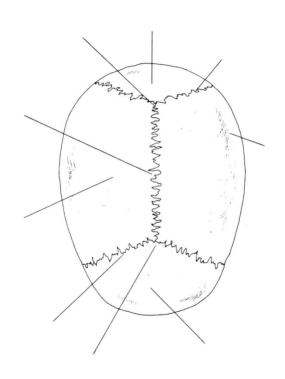

External Skull

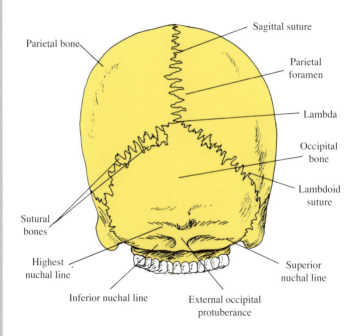

Sagittal suture

Parietal bone

Parietal foramen

Lambda

Occipital bone

Lambdoid suture

Sutural bones

Highest nuchal line

Superior nuchal line

Inferior nuchal line

External occipital protuberance

View: Posterior

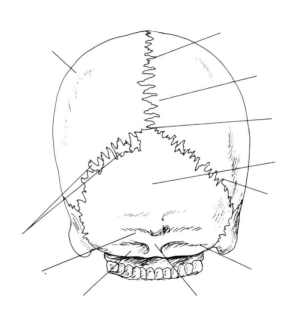

External Skull
(Base)

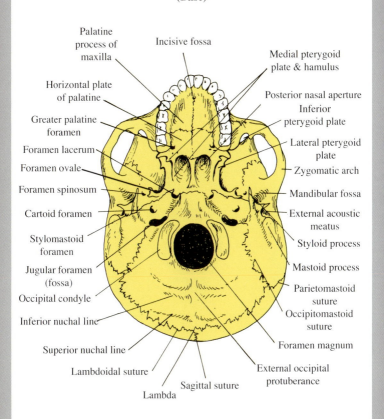

Palatine process of maxilla

Incisive fossa

Medial pterygoid plate & hamulus

Horizontal plate of palatine

Posterior nasal aperture

Inferior pterygoid plate

Greater palatine foramen

Foramen lacerum

Lateral pterygoid plate

Foramen ovale

Zygomatic arch

Foramen spinosum

Mandibular fossa

Cartoid foramen

External acoustic meatus

Stylomastoid foramen

Styloid process

Jugular foramen (fossa)

Mastoid process

Occipital condyle

Parietomastoid suture

Inferior nuchal line

Occipitomastoid suture

Superior nuchal line

Foramen magnum

Lambdoidal suture

External occipital protuberance

Sagittal suture

Lambda

8

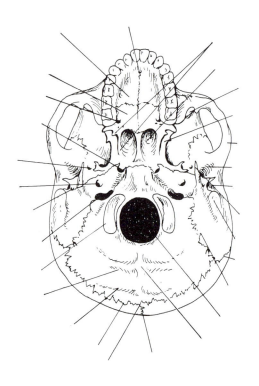

External Skull
(Anterior portion of base)

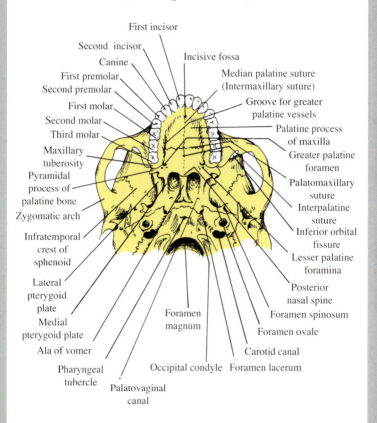

First incisor

Second incisor

Canine

First premolar

Second premolar

First molar

Second molar

Third molar

Maxillary
tuberosity

Pyramidal
process of
palatine bone

Zygomatic arch

Infratemporal
crest of
sphenoid

Lateral
pterygoid
plate

Medial
pterygoid plate

Ala of vomer

Pharyngeal
tubercle

Palatovaginal
canal

Incisive fossa

Median palatine suture
(Intermaxillary suture)

Groove for greater
palatine vessels

Palatine process
of maxilla

Greater palatine
foramen

Palatomaxillary
suture

Interpalatine
suture

Inferior orbital
fissure

Lesser palatine
foramina

Posterior
nasal spine

Foramen spinosum

Foramen ovale

Carotid canal

Foramen lacerum

Occipital condyle

Foramen
magnum

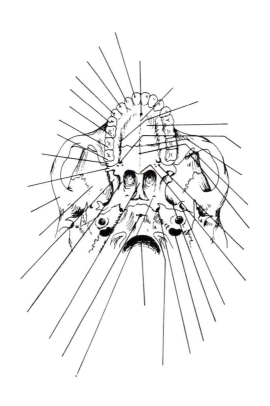

Internal Skull Cap

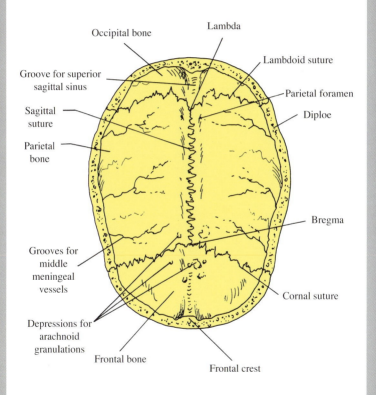

Occipital bone

Lambda

Lambdoid suture

Groove for superior
sagittal sinus

Parietal foramen

Sagittal
suture

Diploe

Parietal
bone

Bregma

Grooves for
middle
meningeal
vessels

Cornal suture

Depressions for
arachnoid
granulations

Frontal bone

Frontal crest

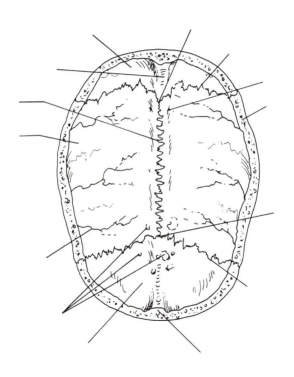

Internal Skull Base
(Cranial fossae)

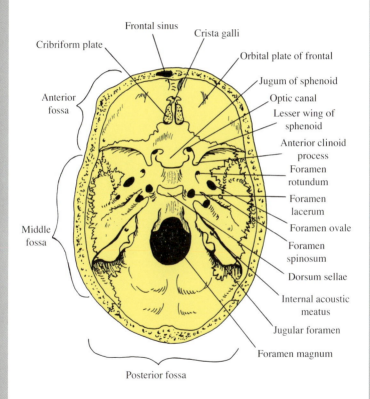

Frontal sinus

Crista galli

Cribriform plate

Orbital plate of frontal

Anterior fossa

Jugum of sphenoid

Optic canal

Lesser wing of sphenoid

Anterior clinoid process

Foramen rotundum

Foramen lacerum

Foramen ovale

Middle fossa

Foramen spinosum

Dorsum sellae

Internal acoustic meatus

Jugular foramen

Foramen magnum

Posterior fossa

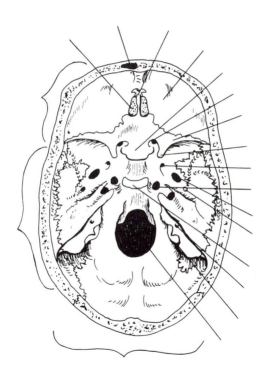

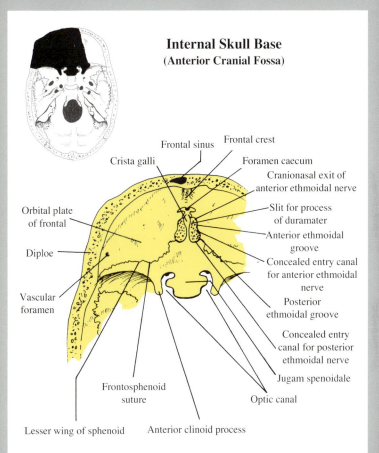

Internal Skull Base
(Anterior Cranial Fossa)

Frontal sinus

Frontal crest

Crista galli

Foramen caecum

Cranionasal exit of anterior ethmoidal nerve

Orbital plate of frontal

Slit for process of duramater

Anterior ethmoidal groove

Diploe

Concealed entry canal for anterior ethmoidal nerve

Posterior ethmoidal groove

Vascular foramen

Concealed entry canal for posterior ethmoidal nerve

Jugam spenoidale

Frontosphenoid suture

Optic canal

Lesser wing of sphenoid

Anterior clinoid process

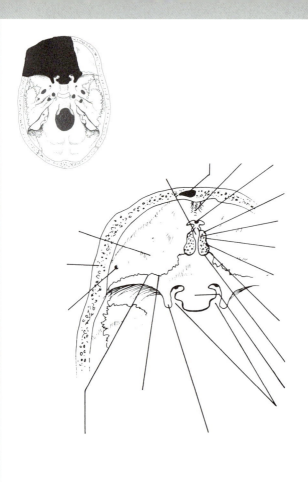

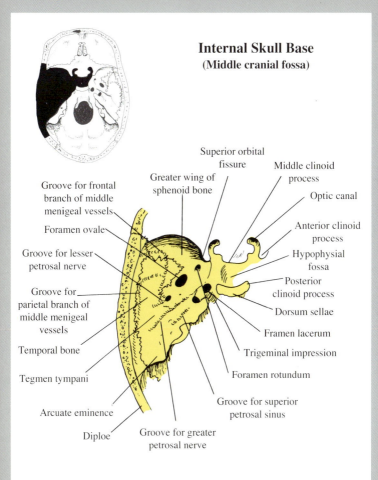

Internal Skull Base
(Middle cranial fossa)

Groove for frontal branch of middle menigeal vessels

Foramen ovale

Groove for lesser petrosal nerve

Groove for parietal branch of middle menigeal vessels

Temporal bone

Tegmen tympani

Arcuate eminence

Diploe

Groove for greater petrosal nerve

Greater wing of sphenoid bone

Superior orbital fissure

Middle clinoid process

Optic canal

Anterior clinoid process

Hypophysial fossa

Posterior clinoid process

Dorsum sellae

Framen lacerum

Trigeminal impression

Foramen rotundum

Groove for superior petrosal sinus

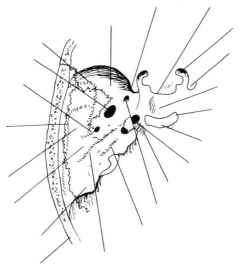

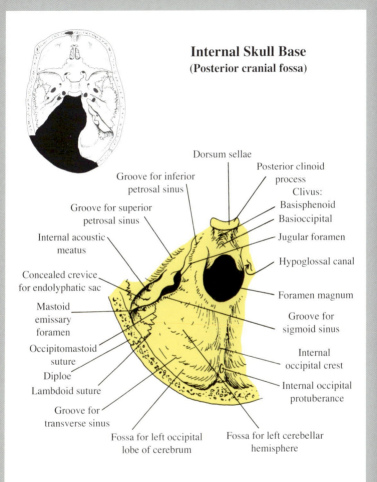

Internal Skull Base
(Posterior cranial fossa)

- Dorsum sellae
- Posterior clinoid process
- Clivus:
  - Basisphenoid
  - Basiocciptal
- Groove for inferior petrosal sinus
- Groove for superior petrosal sinus
- Internal acoustic meatus
- Concealed crevice for endolyphatic sac
- Mastoid emissary foramen
- Occipitomastoid suture
- Diploe
- Lambdoid suture
- Groove for transverse sinus
- Fossa for left occipital lobe of cerebrum
- Jugular foramen
- Hypoglossal canal
- Foramen magnum
- Groove for sigmoid sinus
- Internal occipital crest
- Internal occipital protuberance
- Fossa for left cerebellar hemisphere

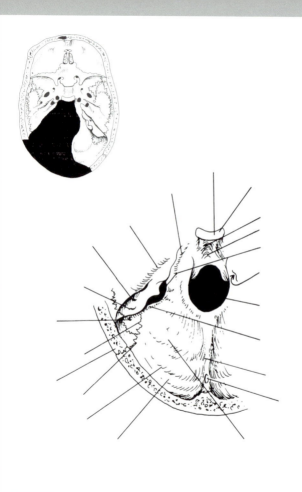

Orbital Cavity and Maxillary Sinus
(Sagittal section of the skull)

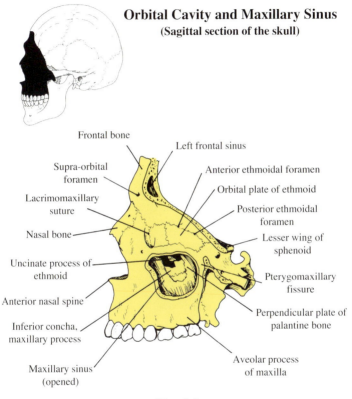

Frontal bone

Left frontal sinus

Supra-orbital foramen

Anterior ethmoidal foramen

Lacrimomaxillary suture

Orbital plate of ethmoid

Nasal bone

Posterior ethmoidal foramen

Uncinate process of ethmoid

Lesser wing of sphenoid

Anterior nasal spine

Pterygomaxillary fissure

Inferior concha, maxillary process

Perpendicular plate of palantine bone

Maxillary sinus (opened)

Aveolar process of maxilla

View: Left

Note: The maxillary opening shows the medial wall of the left maxillary sinus.

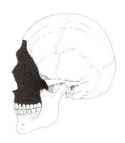

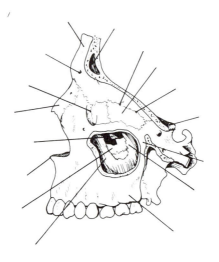

Bony Nasal Septum
(Sagittal section)

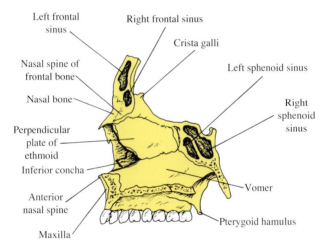

Left frontal sinus

Right frontal sinus

Crista galli

Left sphenoid sinus

Nasal spine of frontal bone

Right sphenoid sinus

Nasal bone

Perpendicular plate of ethmoid

Inferior concha

Vomer

Anterior nasal spine

Pterygoid hamulus

Maxilla

View: Left

Note: This section is to the left of the septum. You are looking at the left side of the septum.

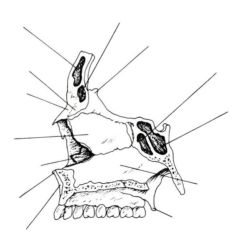

Nasal Cavity
(Sagittal section of the right nasal cavity)

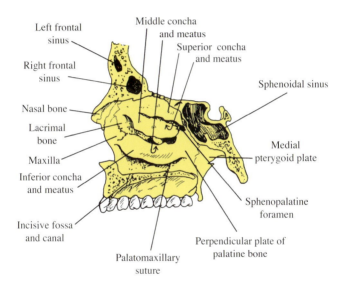

Left frontal sinus

Right frontal sinus

Nasal bone

Lacrimal bone

Maxilla

Inferior concha and meatus

Incisive fossa and canal

Palatomaxillary suture

Middle concha and meatus

Superior concha and meatus

Sphenoidal sinus

Medial pterygoid plate

Sphenopalatine foramen

Perpendicular plate of palatine bone

View: Medial

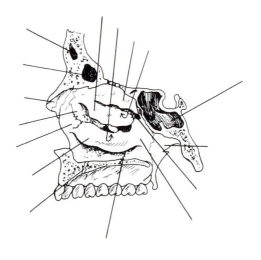

Nasal Cavity Dissected
(Sagittal section of the right nasal cavity)

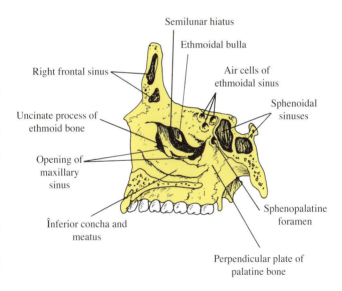

Semilunar hiatus

Ethmoidal bulla

Right frontal sinus

Air cells of
ethmoidal sinus

Sphenoidal
sinuses

Uncinate process of
ethmoid bone

Opening of
maxillary
sinus

Sphenopalatine
foramen

Înferior concha and
meatus

Perpendicular plate of
palatine bone

Note: The middle and superior nasal conchae have been dissected away.

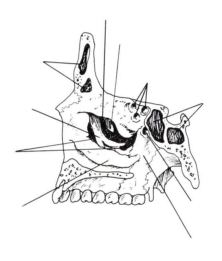

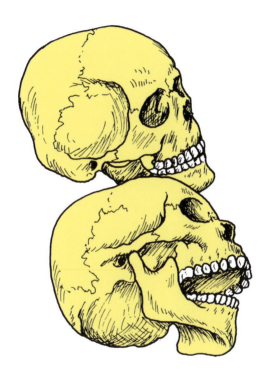

19

Individual Bones of the Skull

Mandible

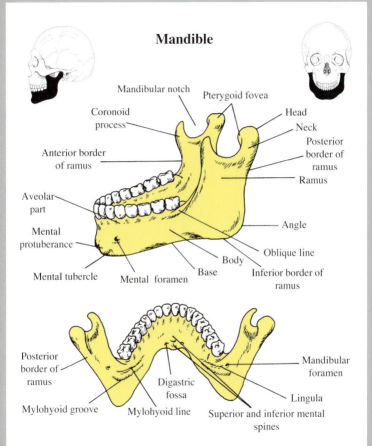

Mandibular notch

Pterygoid fovea

Coronoid process

Head

Neck

Posterior border of ramus

Anterior border of ramus

Ramus

Aveolar part

Mental protuberance

Angle

Oblique line

Body

Mental tubercle

Mental foramen

Base

Inferior border of ramus

Posterior border of ramus

Mandibular foramen

Digastric fossa

Lingula

Mylohyoid groove

Mylohyoid line

Superior and inferior mental spines

View: Posterior

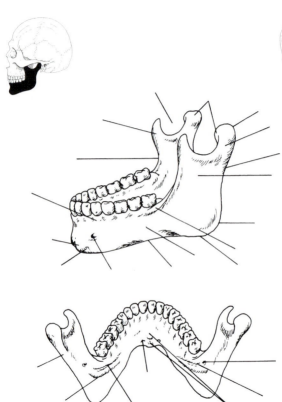

Hyoid Bone

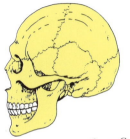

Note: The Hyoid bone is suspended from the tips of the styloid processes of the temporal bones by the stylohyoid ligaments.

Greater horn (cornu)

Lesser horn (cornu)

Body

View: Left lateral

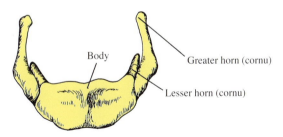

Body

Greater horn (cornu)

Lesser horn (cornu)

View: Superior anterior

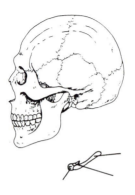

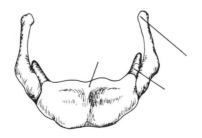

Frontal Bone

Note: See also pages 9, 10, and 11 for internal cranial views of frontal bone.

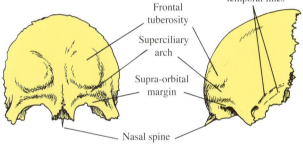

Superior and inferior temporal lines

Frontal tuberosity

Superciliary arch

Supra-orbital margin

Nasal spine

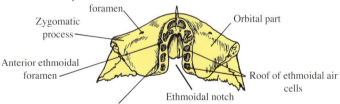

Supra-orbital notch or foramen

Zygomatic process

Anterior ethmoidal foramen

Orbital part

Roof of ethmoidal air cells

Posterior ethmoidal foramen

Ethmoidal notch

View: Inferior

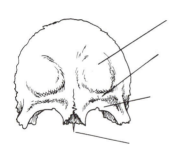
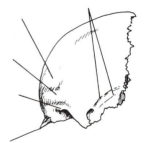
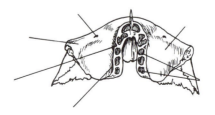

Parietal Bones

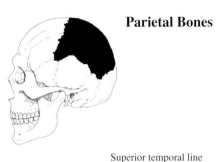

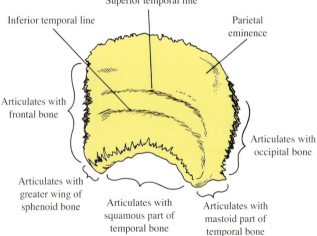

Superior temporal line

Inferior temporal line

Parietal eminence

Articulates with frontal bone

Articulates with occipital bone

Articulates with greater wing of sphenoid bone

Articulates with squamous part of temporal bone

Articulates with mastoid part of temporal bone

View: External

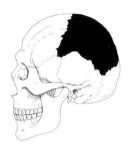

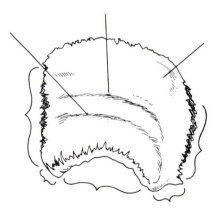

Parietal Bones

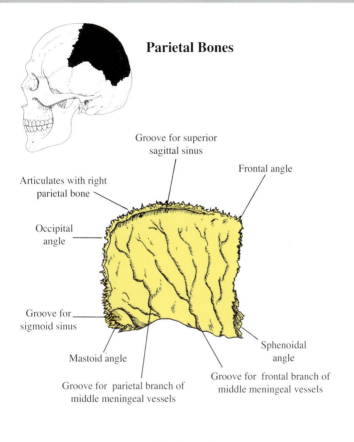

Groove for superior sagittal sinus

Frontal angle

Articulates with right parietal bone

Occipital angle

Groove for sigmoid sinus

Mastoid angle

Sphenoidal angle

Groove for parietal branch of middle meningeal vessels

Groove for frontal branch of middle meningeal vessels

View: Internal

24

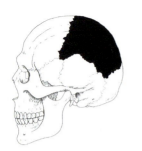

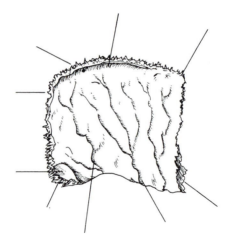

Temporal Bones

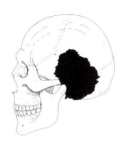
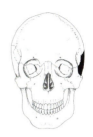

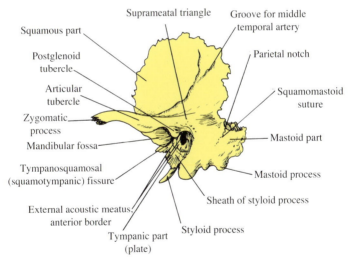

Suprameatal triangle

Groove for middle temporal artery

Squamous part

Parietal notch

Postglenoid tubercle

Squamomastoid suture

Articular tubercle

Zygomatic process

Mastoid part

Mandibular fossa

Mastoid process

Tympanosquamosal (squamotympanic) fissure

Sheath of styloid process

External acoustic meatus: anterior border

Styloid process

Tympanic part (plate)

View: *External*

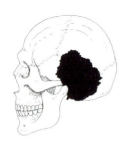

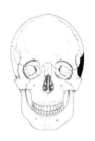

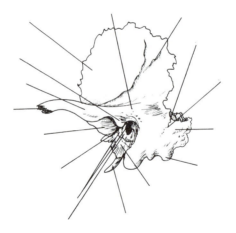

Temporal Bones

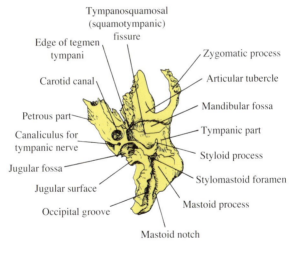

Tympanosquamosal
(squamotympanic)
fissure

Edge of tegmen
tympani

Carotid canal

Petrous part

Canaliculus for
tympanic nerve

Jugular fossa

Jugular surface

Occipital groove

Zygomatic process

Articular tubercle

Mandibular fossa

Tympanic part

Styloid process

Stylomastoid foramen

Mastoid process

Mastoid notch

View: Inferior

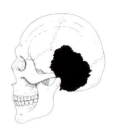

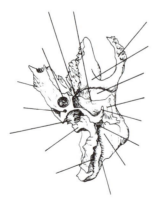

Temporal Bones

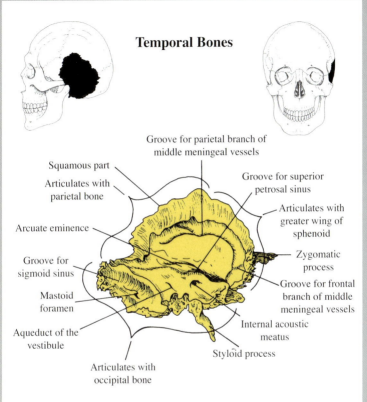

Groove for parietal branch of middle meningeal vessels

Squamous part

Articulates with parietal bone

Groove for superior petrosal sinus

Articulates with greater wing of sphenoid

Arcuate eminence

Zygomatic process

Groove for sigmoid sinus

Groove for frontal branch of middle meningeal vessels

Mastoid foramen

Internal acoustic meatus

Aqueduct of the vestibule

Styloid process

Articulates with occipital bone

View: Internal

Note: See also pages 10, 12, and 13 for further internal cranial views of temporal bone.

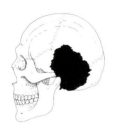

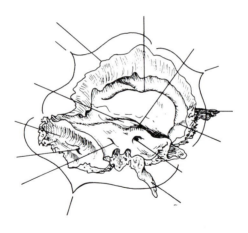

Occipital Bone

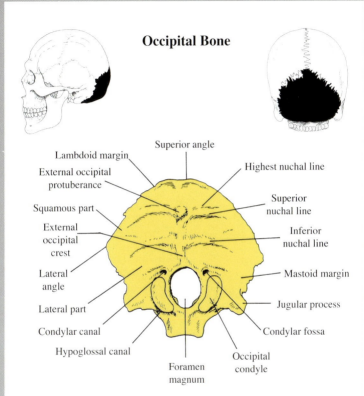

Superior angle

Lambdoid margin

Highest nuchal line

External occipital protuberance

Superior nuchal line

Squamous part

Inferior nuchal line

External occipital crest

Lateral angle

Mastoid margin

Lateral part

Jugular process

Condylar canal

Condylar fossa

Hypoglossal canal

Occipital condyle

Foramen magnum

View: External

Note: There is always a condylar fossa but there may not be a canal.

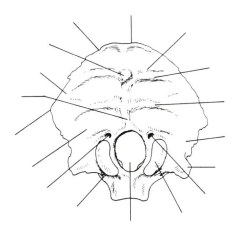

Occipital Bone

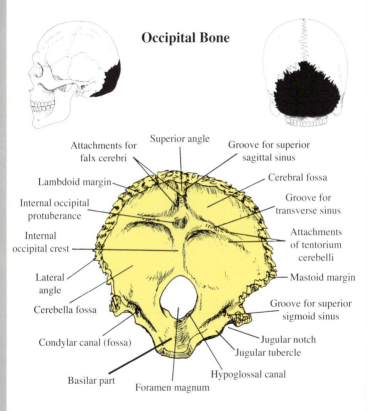

Attachments for falx cerebri

Superior angle

Groove for superior sagittal sinus

Lambdoid margin

Cerebral fossa

Internal occipital protuberance

Groove for transverse sinus

Internal occipital crest

Attachments of tentorium cerebelli

Lateral angle

Mastoid margin

Cerebella fossa

Groove for superior sigmoid sinus

Condylar canal (fossa)

Jugular notch

Jugular tubercle

Basilar part

Hypoglossal canal

Foramen magnum

View: *Internal*

Note: See also cards 10 and 13 for further internal cranial view of occipital bone.

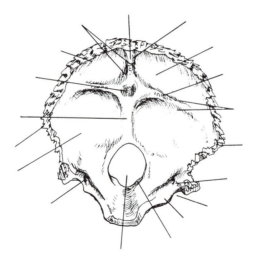

Maxillae Bones

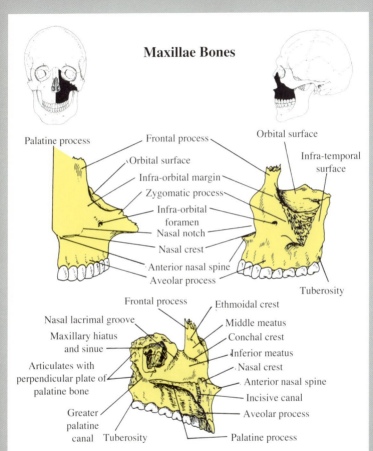

Palatine process

Frontal process

Orbital surface

Orbital surface

Infra-temporal surface

Infra-orbital margin

Zygomatic process

Infra-orbital foramen

Nasal notch

Nasal crest

Anterior nasal spine

Aveolar process

Tuberosity

Frontal process

Ethmoidal crest

Nasal lacrimal groove

Middle meatus

Maxillary hiatus and sinue

Conchal crest

Inferior meatus

Articulates with perpendicular plate of palatine bone

Nasal crest

Anterior nasal spine

Incisive canal

Aveolar process

Greater palatine canal

Tuberosity

Palatine process

View: Medial

Note: See also pages 7 and 8 for inferior views of maxillae bones.

30

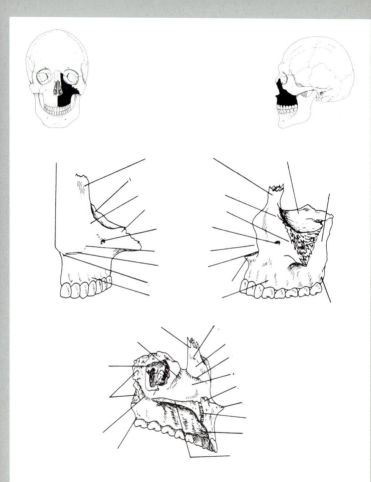

Zygomatic Bones

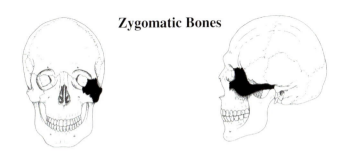

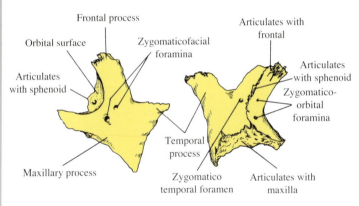

Frontal process

Orbital surface

Zygomaticofacial foramina

Articulates with sphenoid

Maxillary process

Articulates with frontal

Articulates with sphenoid

Zygomatico-orbital foramina

Temporal process

Zygomatico temporal foramen

Articulates with maxilla

View: *Anterolateral*   *View:* *Posteromedial*

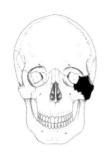
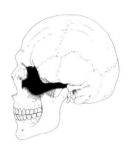
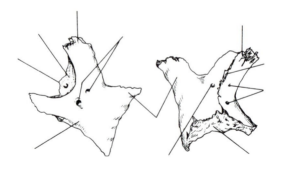

Sphenoid Bone

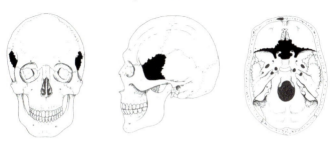

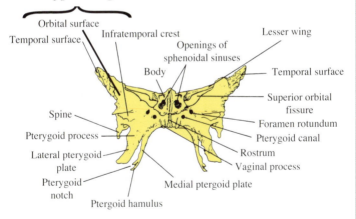

of greater wing

Orbital surface

Temporal surface

Infratemporal crest

Openings of
sphenoidal sinuses

Body

Lesser wing

Temporal surface

Superior orbital
fissure

Foramen rotundum

Pterygoid canal

Rostrum

Vaginal process

Spine

Pterygoid process

Lateral pterygoid
plate

Pterygoid
notch

Ptergoid hamulus

Medial ptergoid plate

View: *Anterior*

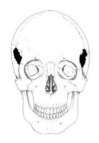
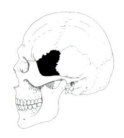
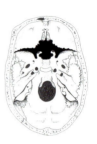
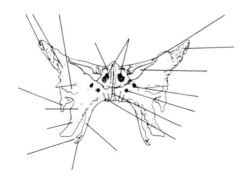

Sphenoid Bone

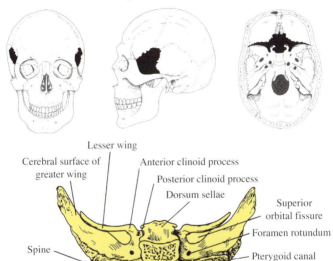

Lesser wing

Cerebral surface of greater wing

Anterior clinoid process

Posterior clinoid process

Dorsum sellae

Superior orbital fissure

Foramen rotundum

Spine

Scaphoid fossa

Lateral pterygoid plate

Pterygoid canal

Vaginal process

Rostrum

Pterygoid notch

Pterygoid hamulus

Medial pterygoid plate

View: Posterior

Note: See also pages 10, 11 and 12 for further internal cranial views of sphenoid bone.

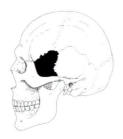

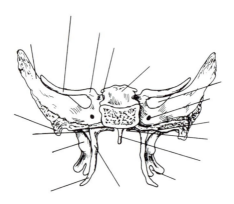

Nasal Bones

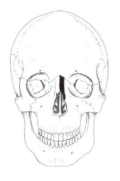
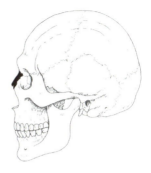

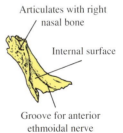

Articulates with frontal

Venous
foramen

Articulates
with maxilla

Notch for
external nasal
nerve

External surface

Articulates with right
nasal bone

Internal surface

Groove for anterior
ethmoidal nerve

View: External

View: Internal

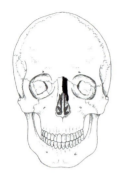
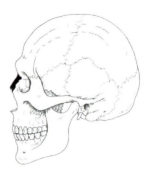

Ethmoid Bone

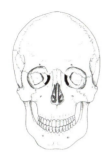

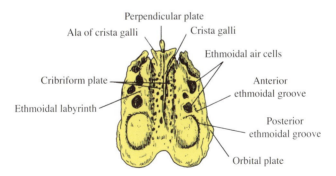

Perpendicular plate

Ala of crista galli   Crista galli

Ethmoidal air cells

Cribriform plate

Anterior
ethmoidal groove

Ethmoidal labyrinth

Posterior
ethmoidal groove

Orbital plate

View: Superior

35

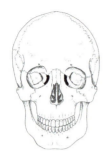 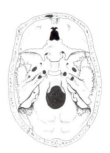

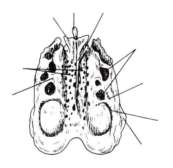

Ethmoid Bone

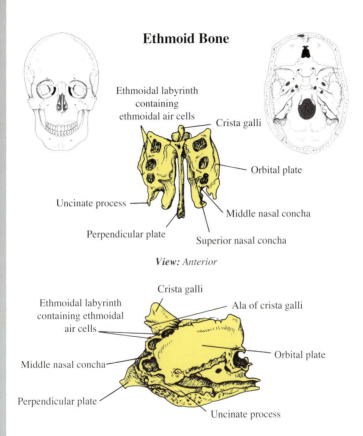

Ethmoidal labyrinth containing ethmoidal air cells

Crista galli

Orbital plate

Uncinate process

Middle nasal concha

Perpendicular plate

Superior nasal concha

View: Anterior

Crista galli

Ala of crista galli

Ethmoidal labyrinth containing ethmoidal air cells

Orbital plate

Middle nasal concha

Perpendicular plate

Uncinate process

View: Left lateral

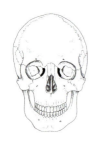

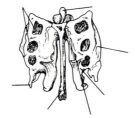

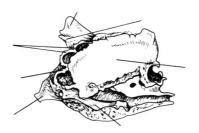

Vomer Bone

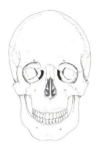

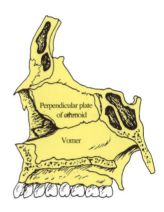

Perpendicular plate of ethmoid

Vomer

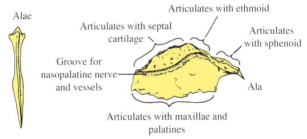

Alae

Articulates with ethmoid

Articulates with septal cartilage

Articulates with sphenoid

Groove for nasopalatine nerve and vessels

Ala

Articulates with maxillae and palatines

View: *Posterior inferior*

View: *Left lateral*

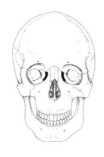

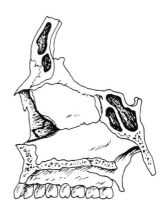

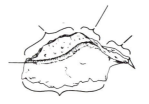

Palatine Bones

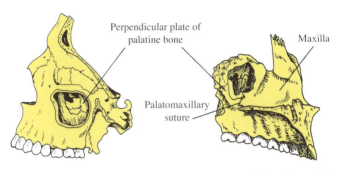

Perpendicular plate of palatine bone

Maxilla

Palatomaxillary suture

Sagittal section of skull showing the medial wall of left maxillary sinus.

Medial view of left maxilla and left palatine bones articulated.

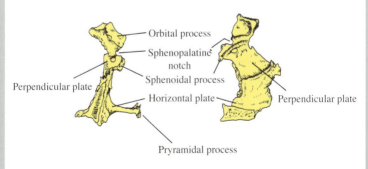

Orbital process

Sphenopalatine notch

Perpendicular plate

Sphenoidal process

Horizontal plate

Perpendicular plate

Pryramidal process

View: Posterior

View: Anterior

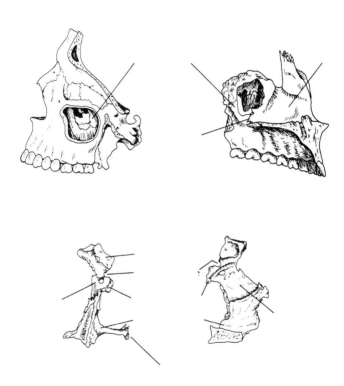

Palatine Bones

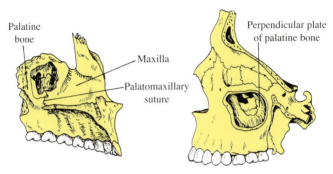

Palatine bone

Maxilla

Palatomaxillary suture

Perpendicular plate of palatine bone

Medial view of left maxilla and palatine bones articulated.

Sagittal section of the skull showing the medial wall of left maxillary sinus.

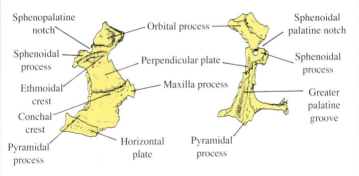

Sphenopalatine notch

Sphenoidal process

Ethmoidal crest

Conchal crest

Pyramidal process

Orbital process

Perpendicular plate

Maxilla process

Horizontal plate

Sphenoidal palatine notch

Sphenoidal process

Greater palatine groove

Pyramidal process

View: Medial

View:Left lateral

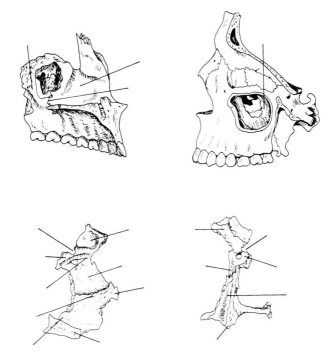

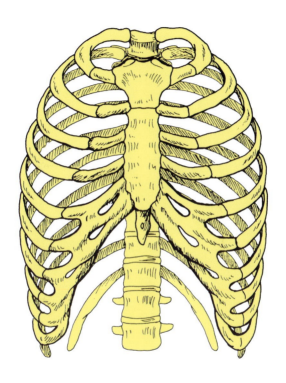

40

Bones of the Vertebral Column and Thorax

Typical Cervical Vertebrae

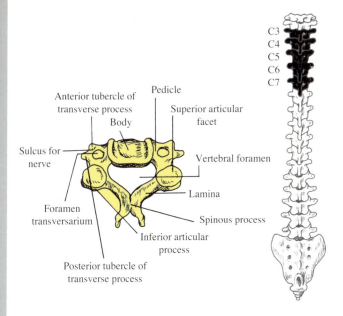

Anterior tubercle of transverse process

Pedicle

Body

Superior articular facet

Sulcus for nerve

Vertebral foramen

Foramen transversarium

Lamina

Spinous process

Inferior articular process

Posterior tubercle of transverse process

C3
C4
C5
C6
C7

View: Superior, posterior

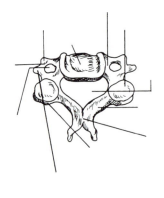

Atlas
First Cervical Vertebra

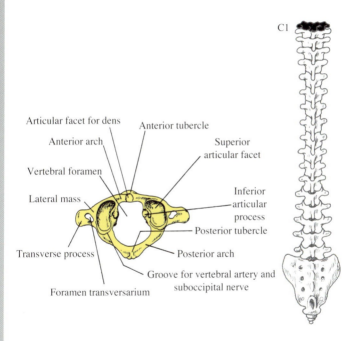

C1

Articular facet for dens

Anterior tubercle

Anterior arch

Superior articular facet

Vertebral foramen

Inferior articular process

Lateral mass

Posterior tubercle

Transverse process

Posterior arch

Foramen transversarium

Groove for vertebral artery and suboccipital nerve

View: Superior, posterior

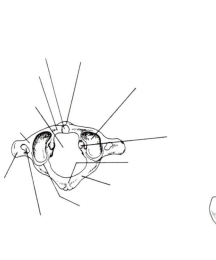

Axis
Second Cervical Vertebra

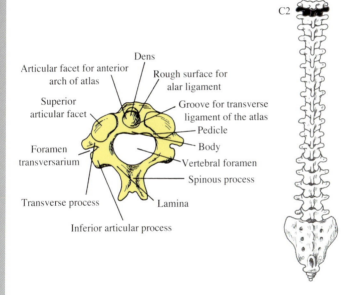

C2

Dens

Articular facet for anterior
arch of atlas

Rough surface for
alar ligament

Superior
articular facet

Groove for transverse
ligament of the atlas

Pedicle

Foramen
transversarium

Body

Vertebral foramen

Spinous process

Transverse process

Lamina

Inferior articular process

View: Superior, posterior

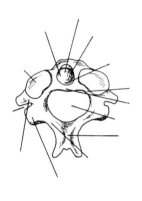

Typical Thoracic Vertebrae

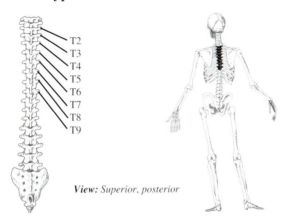

T2
T3
T4
T5
T6
T7
T8
T9

View: *Superior, posterior*

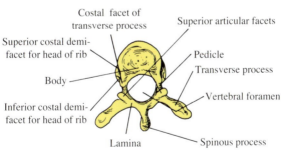

Costal facet of transverse process

Superior costal demi-facet for head of rib

Body

Inferior costal demi-facet for head of rib

Lamina

Superior articular facets

Pedicle

Transverse process

Vertebral foramen

Spinous process

Note: The first, ninth, tenth, eleventh, and twelfth thoracic vertebrae present certain differences, and must be specially considered.

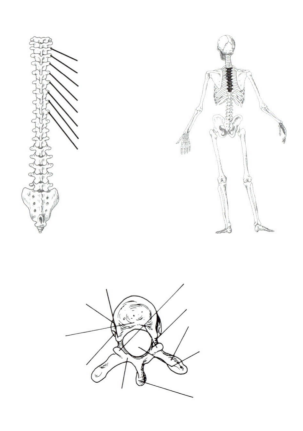

Typical Lumbar Vertebra

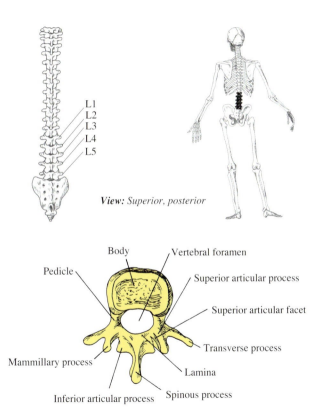

L1
L2
L3
L4
L5

View: Superior, posterior

Body

Vertebral foramen

Pedicle

Superior articular process

Superior articular facet

Transverse process

Mammillary process

Lamina

Inferior articular process

Spinous process

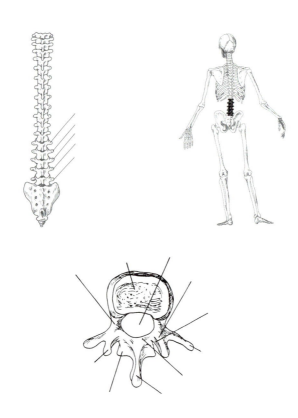

Sacrum and Coccyx

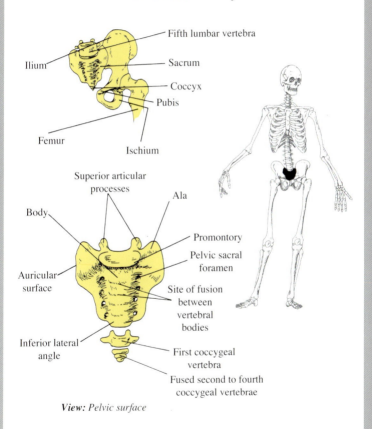

Fifth lumbar vertebra

Ilium

Sacrum

Coccyx

Pubis

Femur

Ischium

Superior articular processes

Ala

Body

Promontory

Pelvic sacral foramen

Auricular surface

Site of fusion between vertebral bodies

Inferior lateral angle

First coccygeal vertebra

Fused second to fourth coccygeal vertebrae

View: Pelvic surface

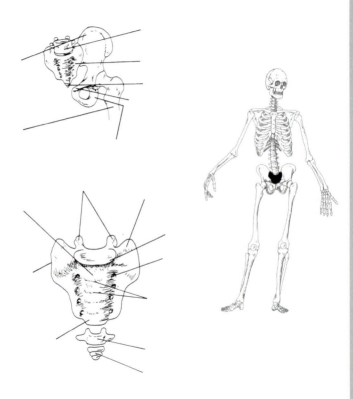

Sacrum and Coccyx

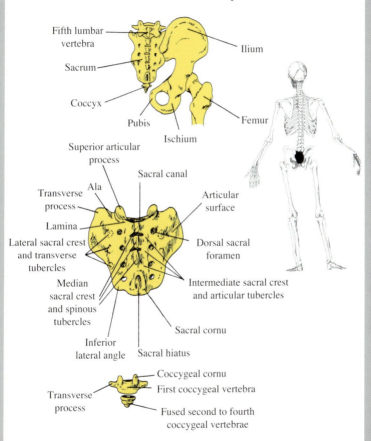

Fifth lumbar vertebra

Ilium

Sacrum

Coccyx

Pubis

Femur

Ischium

Superior articular process

Sacral canal

Ala

Transverse process

Articular surface

Lamina

Lateral sacral crest and transverse tubercles

Dorsal sacral foramen

Median sacral crest and spinous tubercles

Intermediate sacral crest and articular tubercles

Inferior lateral angle

Sacral cornu

Sacral hiatus

Coccygeal cornu

First coccygeal vertebra

Transverse process

Fused second to fourth coccygeal vertebrae

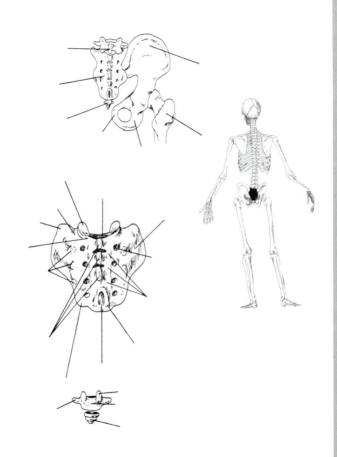

Rib Cage

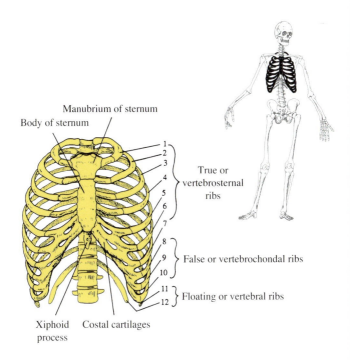

Manubrium of sternum

Body of sternum

1
2
3
4
5
6
7

True or vertebrosternal ribs

8
9
10

False or vertebrochondal ribs

11
12

Floating or vertebral ribs

Xiphoid process

Costal cartilages

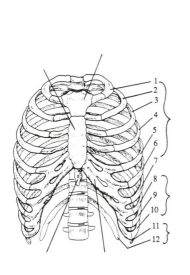
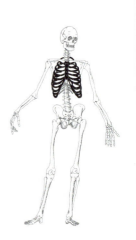

1
2
3
4 }
5
6
7
8 }
9
10 }
11 }
12 }

Sternum

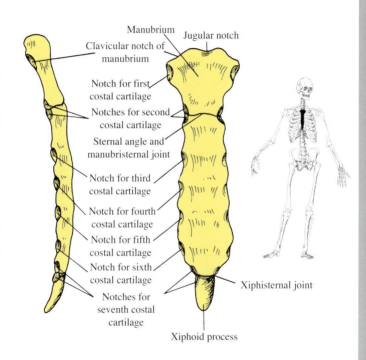

Manubrium

Jugular notch

Clavicular notch of manubrium

Notch for first costal cartilage

Notches for second costal cartilage

Sternal angle and manubristernal joint

Notch for third costal cartilage

Notch for fourth costal cartilage

Notch for fifth costal cartilage

Notch for sixth costal cartilage

Notches for seventh costal cartilage

Xiphisternal joint

Xiphoid process

View: Left side

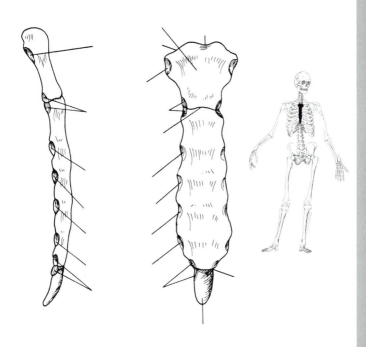

Typical Right Middle Rib

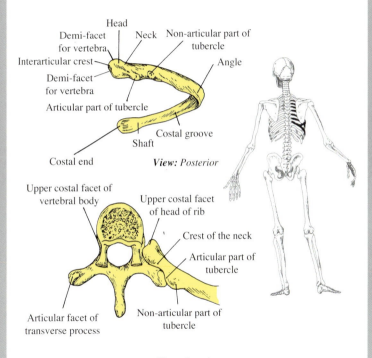

Head

Demi-facet for vertebra

Neck

Non-articular part of tubercle

Interarticular crest

Angle

Demi-facet for vertebra

Articular part of tubercle

Costal groove

Shaft

Costal end

View: Posterior

Upper costal facet of vertebral body

Upper costal facet of head of rib

Crest of the neck

Articular part of tubercle

Non-articular part of tubercle

Articular facet of transverse process

View: Superior

Note: Atypical ribs: the first, second, tenth, eleventh and twelfth ribs present certain variations from the common characteristics.

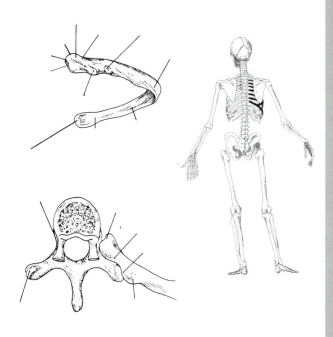

Typical Right Middle Rib

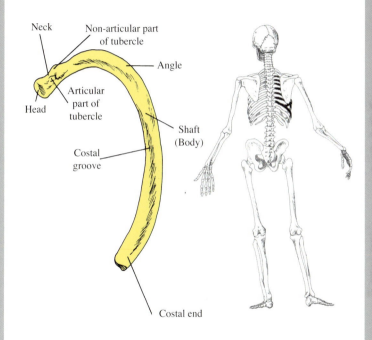

Neck

Non-articular part
of tubercle

Angle

Articular
part of
tubercle

Head

Shaft
(Body)

Costal
groove

Costal end

View: Inferior

Note: Atypical ribs: the first, second, tenth, eleventh and twelfth ribs present certain variations from the common characteristics.

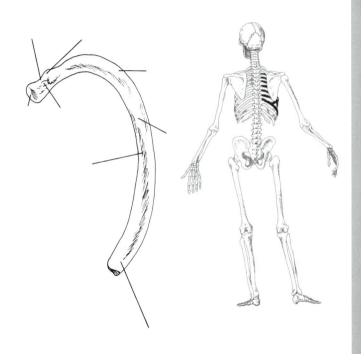

First and Second Ribs
(Atypical Ribs)

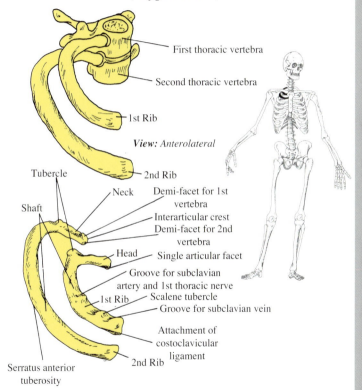

First thoracic vertebra

Second thoracic vertebra

1st Rib

View: Anterolateral

2nd Rib

Tubercle

Neck

Shaft

Demi-facet for 1st
vertebra

Interarticular crest

Demi-facet for 2nd
vertebra

Head

Single articular facet

Groove for subclavian
artery and 1st thoracic nerve

1st Rib

Scalene tubercle

Groove for subclavian vein

Attachment of
costoclavicular
ligament

2nd Rib

Serratus anterior
tuberosity

View: Superior

52

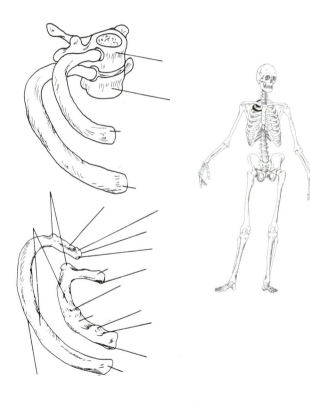

Tenth, Eleventh and Twelfth Ribs
(Atypical Ribs)

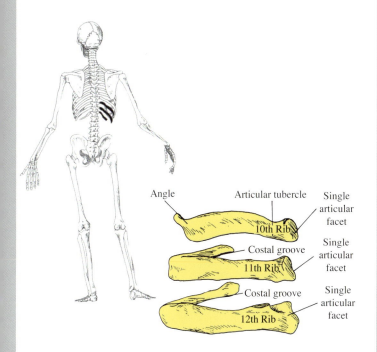

Angle

Articular tubercle

Single articular facet

10th Rib

Costal groove

Single articular facet

11th Rib

Costal groove

Single articular facet

12th Rib

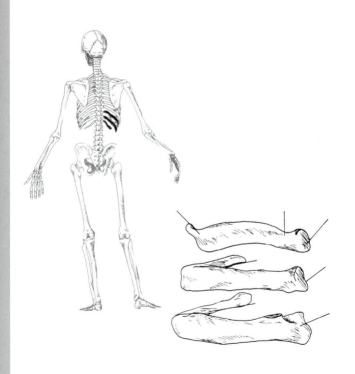

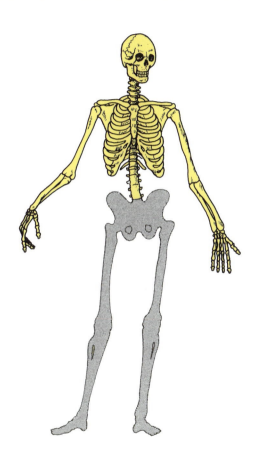

Bones of the Upper Appendicular Skeleton

Scapula and Clavicle

View: Anterior

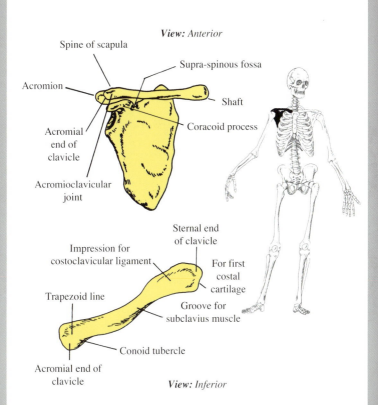

Spine of scapula

Supra-spinous fossa

Acromion

Shaft

Acromial end of clavicle

Coracoid process

Acromioclavicular joint

Sternal end of clavicle

Impression for costoclavicular ligament

For first costal cartilage

Trapezoid line

Groove for subclavius muscle

Conoid tubercle

Acromial end of clavicle

View: Inferior

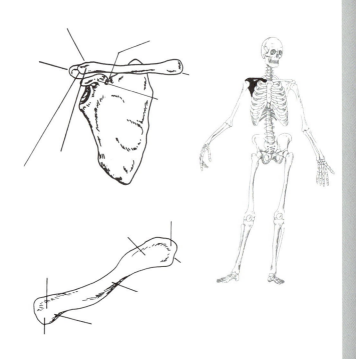

Scapula

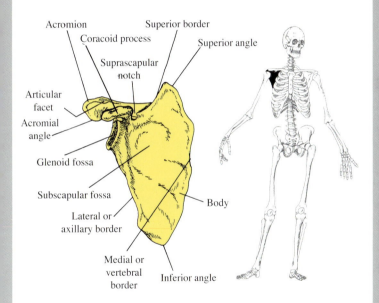

Acromion

Coracoid process

Superior border

Superior angle

Suprascapular notch

Articular facet

Acromial angle

Glenoid fossa

Subscapular fossa

Lateral or axillary border

Body

Medial or vertebral border

Inferior angle

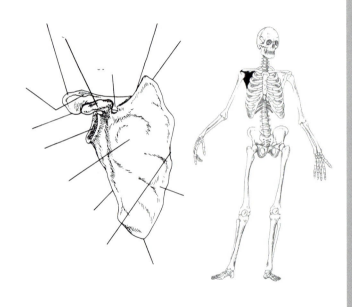

Scapula

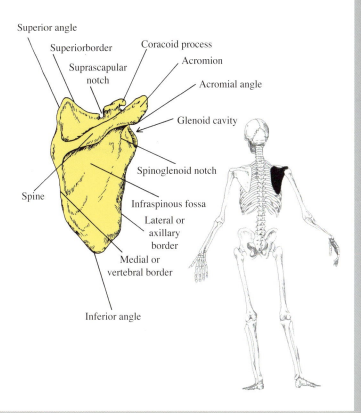

Superior angle

Superiorborder

Suprascapular notch

Coracoid process

Acromion

Acromial angle

Glenoid cavity

Spinoglenoid notch

Spine

Infraspinous fossa

Lateral or axillary border

Medial or vertebral border

Inferior angle

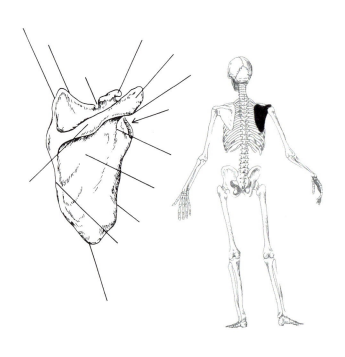

Humerus

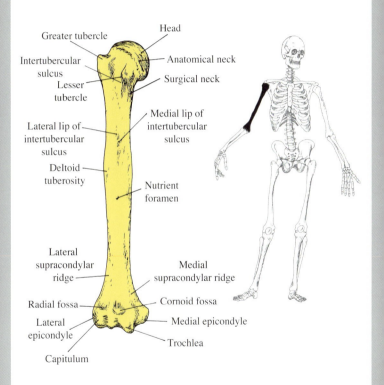

Greater tubercle

Head

Intertubercular sulcus

Anatomical neck

Lesser tubercle

Surgical neck

Lateral lip of intertubercular sulcus

Medial lip of intertubercular sulcus

Deltoid tuberosity

Nutrient foramen

Lateral supracondylar ridge

Medial supracondylar ridge

Radial fossa

Cornoid fossa

Lateral epicondyle

Medial epicondyle

Capitulum

Trochlea

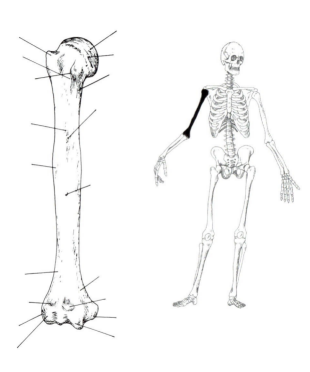

Humerus

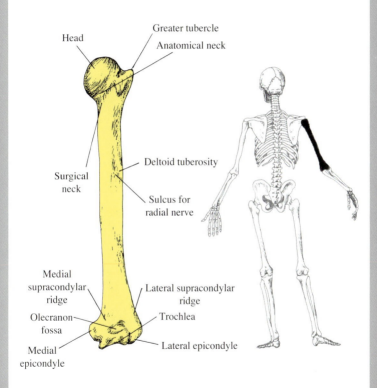

Head

Greater tubercle

Anatomical neck

Surgical neck

Deltoid tuberosity

Sulcus for radial nerve

Medial supracondylar ridge

Lateral supracondylar ridge

Olecranon fossa

Trochlea

Medial epicondyle

Lateral epicondyle

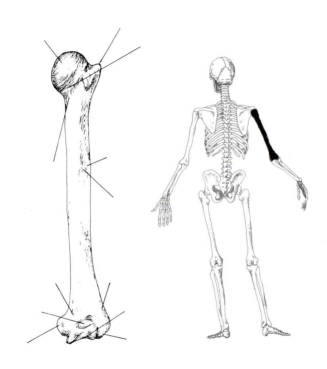

Radius

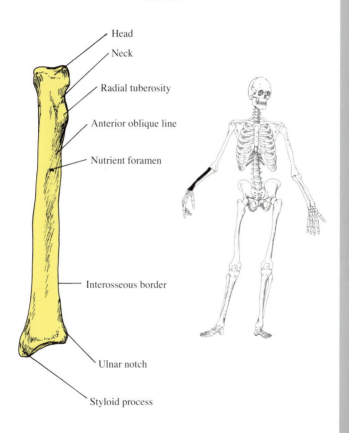

Head

Neck

Radial tuberosity

Anterior oblique line

Nutrient foramen

Interosseous border

Ulnar notch

Styloid process

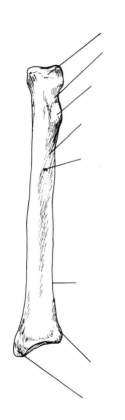
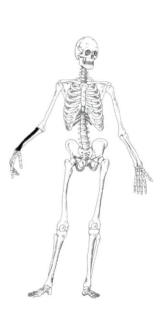

Radius

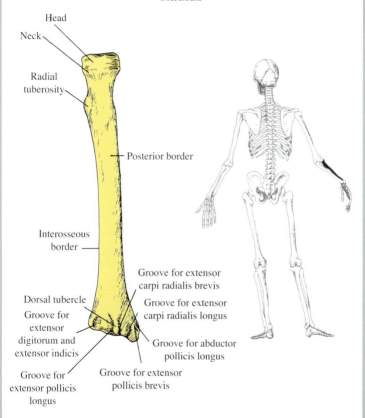

Head

Neck

Radial
tuberosity

Posterior border

Interosseous
border

Dorsal tubercle
Groove for
extensor
digitorum and
extensor indicis

Groove for
extensor pollicis
longus

Groove for extensor
pollicis brevis

Groove for extensor
carpi radialis brevis

Groove for extensor
carpi radialis longus

Groove for abductor
pollicis longus

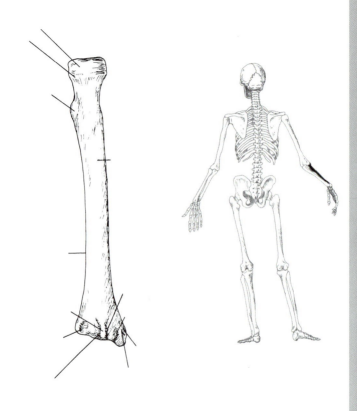

Ulna

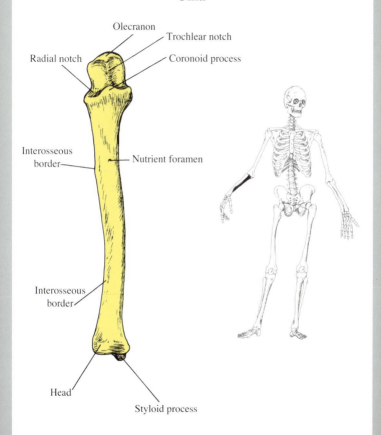

Olecranon

Trochlear notch

Radial notch

Coronoid process

Interosseous border

Nutrient foramen

Interosseous border

Head

Styloid process

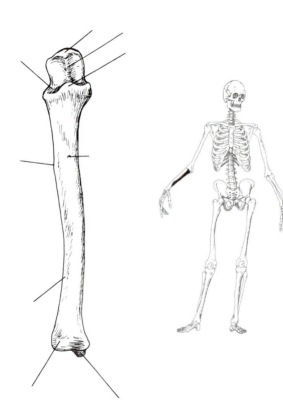

Ulna

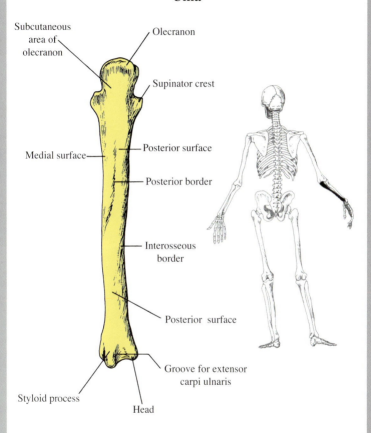

Subcutaneous area of olecranon

Olecranon

Supinator crest

Medial surface

Posterior surface

Posterior border

Interosseous border

Posterior surface

Styloid process

Head

Groove for extensor carpi ulnaris

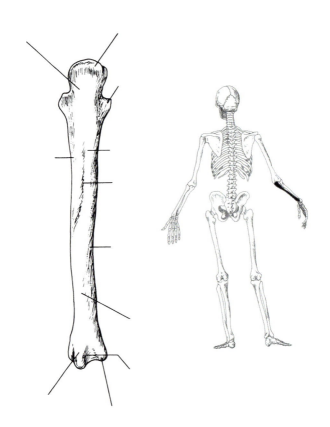

Carpus and Metacarpus

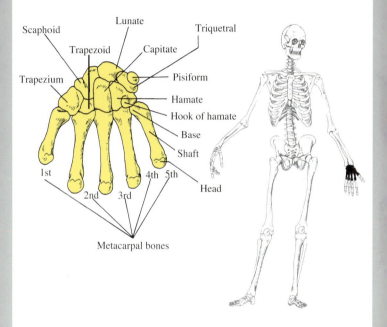

Scaphoid

Lunate

Triquetral

Trapezoid

Capitate

Trapezium

Pisiform

Hamate

Hook of hamate

Base

Shaft

1st

4th 5th

2nd

3rd

Head

Metacarpal bones

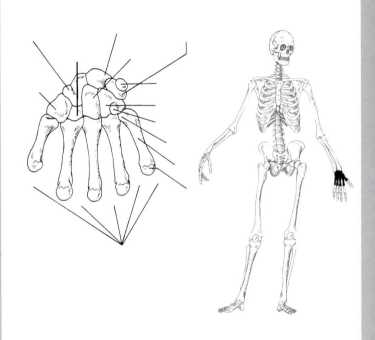

Carpus and Metacarpus

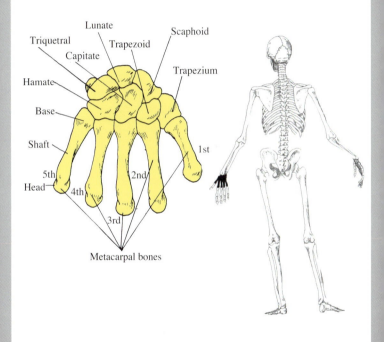

Lunate

Triquetral

Trapezoid

Scaphoid

Capitate

Trapezium

Hamate

Base

Shaft

1st

5th

2nd

Head

4th

3rd

Metacarpal bones

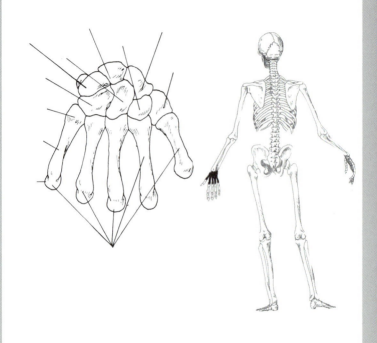

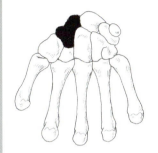
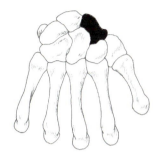

Scaphoid Bone

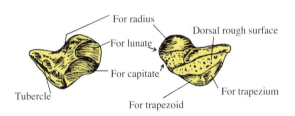

For radius

For lunate

Dorsal rough surface

For capitate

Tubercle

For trapezium

For trapezoid

View: *Palmar*

View: *Dorsal*

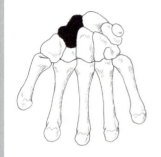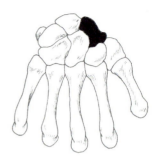

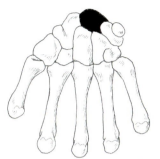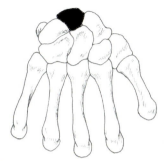

Lunate Bone

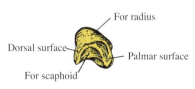

For hamate — Palmar surface

For capitate — For triquetral

Dorsal surface

View: Dorso medial

For radius

Dorsal surface — Palmar surface

For scaphoid

View: Proximal lateral

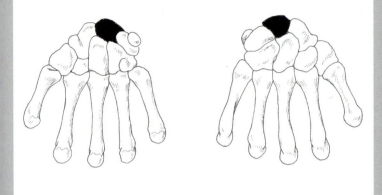

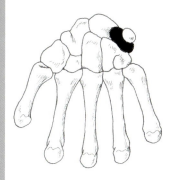
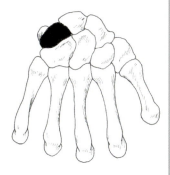

Triquetral Bone

For lunate bone

For pisiform bone

For hamate bone

For lunate bone

For hamate bone

View: Palmar

View: Dorsal

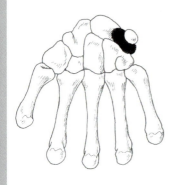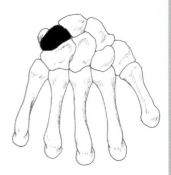

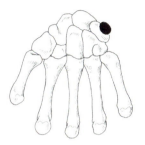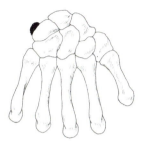

Pisiform Bone

For triquetral bone

View: *Dorsal*

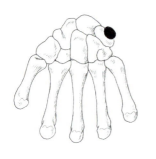 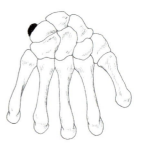

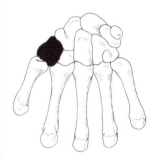 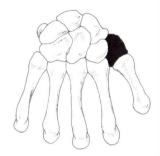

Trapezium Bone

Tubercle — For scaphoid

Groove for flexor
carpi radialis tendon

For trapezoid

For 1st
metacarpal

For 2nd metacarpal

View: Palmar

For scaphoid — For trapezoid

Lateral surface — For 2nd metacarpal

Groove for flexor
carpi radialis tendon

Tubercle

View: Proximomedial

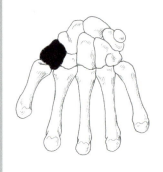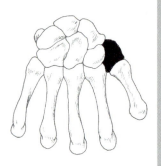

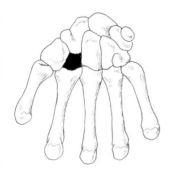
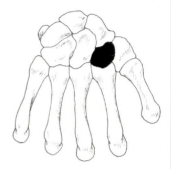

Trapezoid Bone

View: *Medial*

For capitate
Palmar surface
For scaphoid
Dorsal surface
For 2nd metacarpal

For trapezium
Dorsal surface
For scaphoid
Rough palmar surface
For 2nd metacarpal

View: *Lateral*

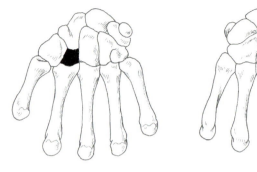
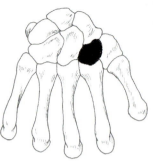

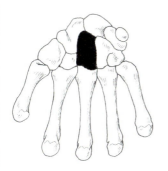
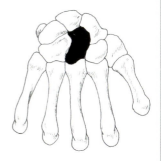

Capitate Bone

For lunate

For hamate — Palmar surface

View: Medial

For 4th metacarpal — For 3rd metacarpal

For scaphoid

View: Lateral

Dorsal surface — For trapezoid

For 3rd metacarpal — For 2nd metacarpal

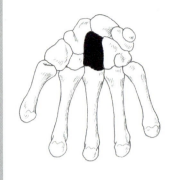
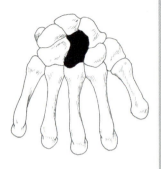

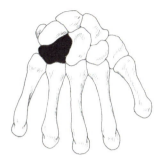

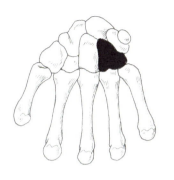

Hamate Bone

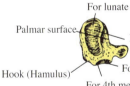

For lunate

Palmar surface

For triquetral

Hook (Hamulus)

For 5th metacarpal

For 4th metacarpal

View: Medial

For lunate

View: Lateral

Dorsal surface

For capitate

For 4th metacarpal

Hook

For 5th metacarpal

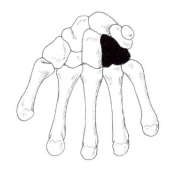
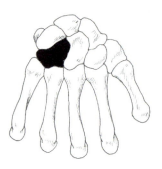

 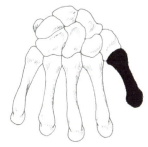

First Metacarpal

For trapezium

Base

Shaft

View: Palmar

Head for
proximal
phalanx

Articular
eminence for
sesamoid bone

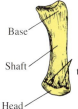

View: Medial

Base

Shaft

Articular eminences for the
two sesamoid bones in the
tendons of the flexor pollicis
brevis

Head

Note: Caution should be exercised when considering descriptions of this bone: topographical terms are used to describe the views rather than morphological.

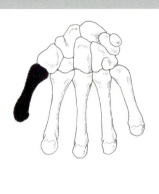

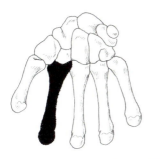 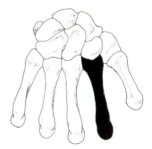

Second Metacarpal

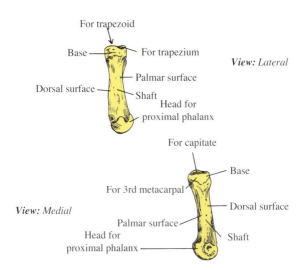

For trapezoid

Base

For trapezium

Palmar surface

Dorsal surface

Shaft

Head for
proximal phalanx

View: Lateral

For capitate

Base

For 3rd metacarpal

Dorsal surface

View: Medial

Palmar surface

Shaft

Head for
proximal phalanx

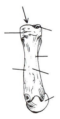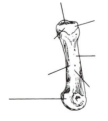

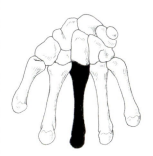
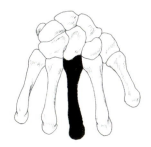

Third Metacarpal

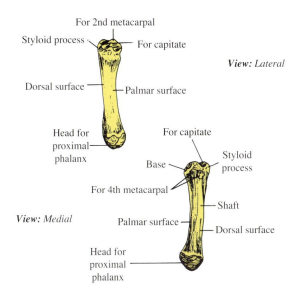

For 2nd metacarpal

Styloid process — For capitate

View: Lateral

Dorsal surface — Palmar surface

Head for
proximal
phalanx

For capitate

Base — Styloid
process

For 4th metacarpal

Shaft

View: Medial

Palmar surface — Dorsal surface

Head for
proximal
phalanx

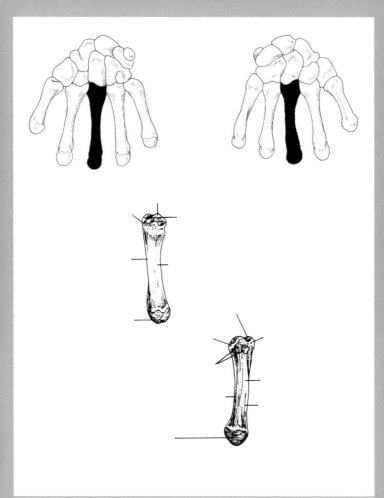

Fourth Metacarpal

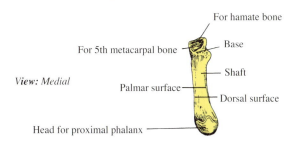

For capitate bone

Base

Shaft

Dorsal surface

For 3rd metacarpal bone

View: Lateral

Palmar surface

Head for proximal phalanx

For hamate bone

For 5th metacarpal bone

Base

View: Medial

Shaft

Palmar surface

Dorsal surface

Head for proximal phalanx

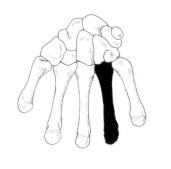
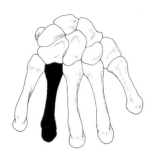

Fifth Metacarpal

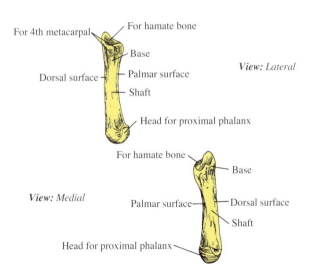

For 4th metacarpal

For hamate bone

Base

Dorsal surface

Palmar surface

Shaft

Head for proximal phalanx

View: *Lateral*

For hamate bone

Base

View: *Medial*

Palmar surface

Dorsal surface

Shaft

Head for proximal phalanx

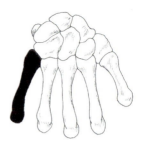

Joints of the Wrist and Hand

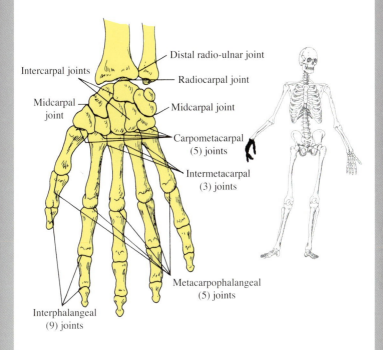

Intercarpal joints

Distal radio-ulnar joint

Radiocarpal joint

Midcarpal joint

Midcarpal joint

Carpometacarpal (5) joints

Intermetacarpal (3) joints

Metacarpophalangeal (5) joints

Interphalangeal (9) joints

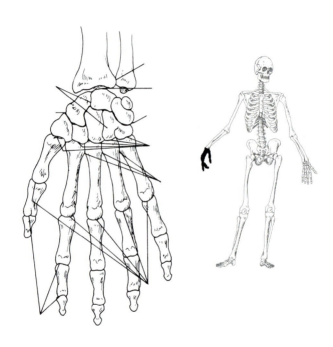

Joints of the Wrist and Hand

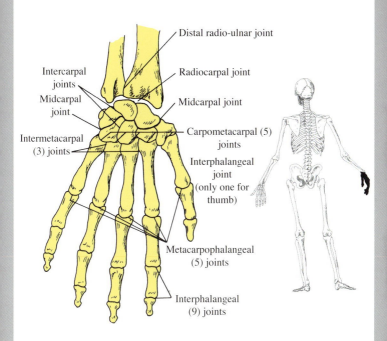

Distal radio-ulnar joint

Intercarpal joints

Radiocarpal joint

Midcarpal joint

Midcarpal joint

Intermetacarpal (3) joints

Carpometacarpal (5) joints

Interphalangeal joint (only one for thumb)

Metacarpophalangeal (5) joints

Interphalangeal (9) joints

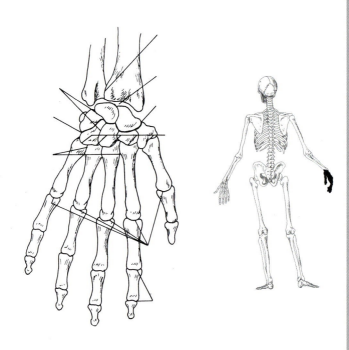

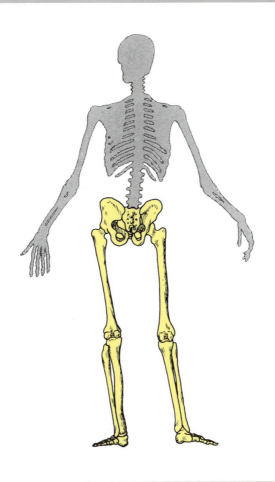

81

Bones of the Lower Appendicular Skeleton

Os Coxae
(Hip Bone)

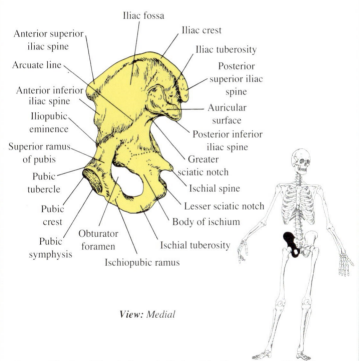

Iliac fossa

Anterior superior
iliac spine

Iliac crest

Iliac tuberosity

Arcuate line

Posterior
superior iliac
spine

Anterior inferior
iliac spine

Iliopubic
eminence

Auricular
surface

Posterior inferior
iliac spine

Superior ramus
of pubis

Greater
sciatic notch

Pubic
tubercle

Ischial spine

Pubic
crest

Lesser sciatic notch

Body of ischium

Obturator
foramen

Ischial tuberosity

Pubic
symphysis

Ischiopubic ramus

View: *Medial*

Note: ....The dotted lines indicate the limits of the iliac, pubic, and ischial parts
of the bone.

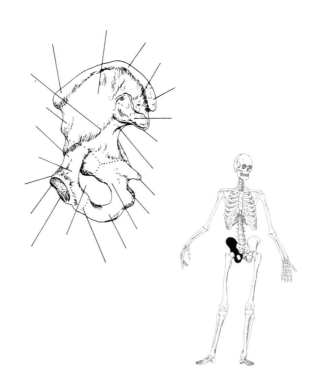

Os Coxae
(Hip Bone)

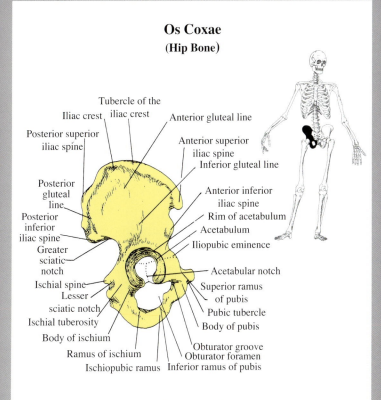

Tubercle of the iliac crest

Iliac crest

Anterior gluteal line

Posterior superior iliac spine

Anterior superior iliac spine

Inferior gluteal line

Posterior gluteal line

Anterior inferior iliac spine

Posterior inferior iliac spine

Rim of acetabulum

Acetabulum

Greater sciatic notch

Iliopubic eminence

Ischial spine

Acetabular notch

Lesser sciatic notch

Superior ramus of pubis

Ischial tuberosity

Pubic tubercle

Body of ischium

Body of pubis

Ramus of ischium

Obturator groove

Ischiopubic ramus

Obturator foramen

Inferior ramus of pubis

View: *Lateral*

Note:....The dotted lines indicate the limits of the iliac, pubic, and ischial parts of the bone.

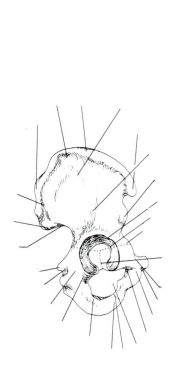
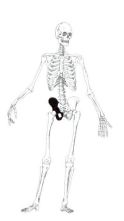

Femur

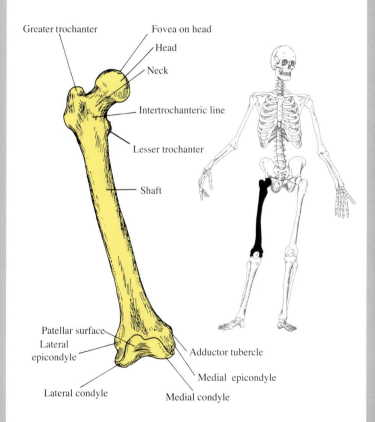

Greater trochanter

Fovea on head

Head

Neck

Intertrochanteric line

Lesser trochanter

Shaft

Patellar surface

Lateral epicondyle

Adductor tubercle

Medial epicondyle

Lateral condyle

Medial condyle

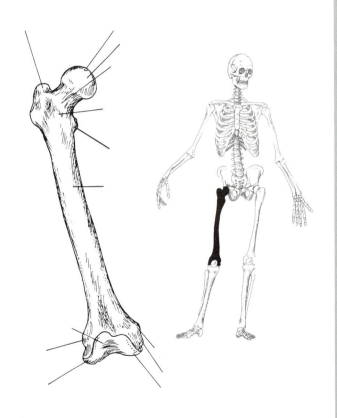

Femur

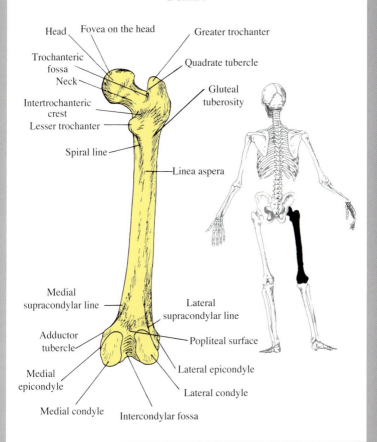

Head

Fovea on the head

Greater trochanter

Trochanteric fossa

Quadrate tubercle

Neck

Gluteal tuberosity

Intertrochanteric crest

Lesser trochanter

Spiral line

Linea aspera

Medial supracondylar line

Lateral supracondylar line

Adductor tubercle

Popliteal surface

Medial epicondyle

Lateral epicondyle

Lateral condyle

Medial condyle

Intercondylar fossa

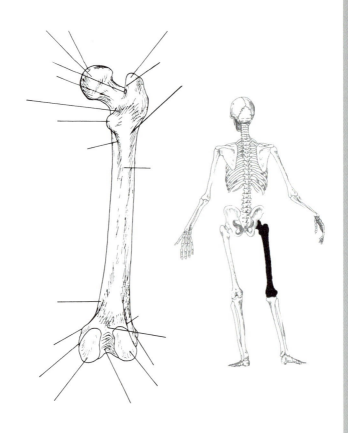

Patella

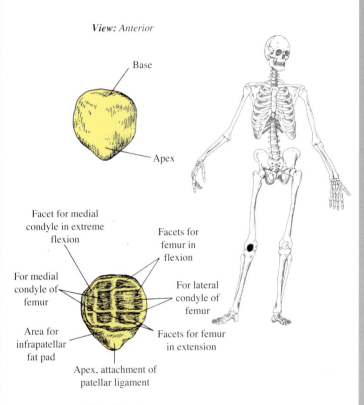

View: *Anterior*

Base

Apex

Facet for medial
condyle in extreme
flexion

Facets for
femur in
flexion

For medial
condyle of
femur

For lateral
condyle of
femur

Area for
infrapatellar
fat pad

Facets for femur
in extension

Apex, attachment of
patellar ligament

View: *Posterior*

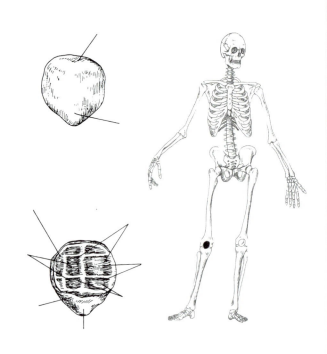

Tibia

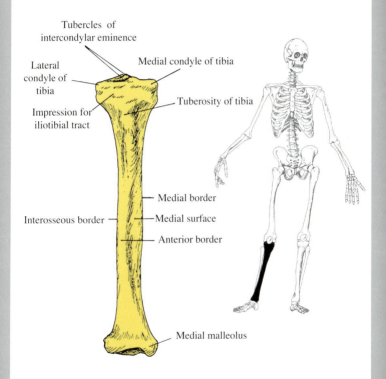

Tubercles of intercondylar eminence

Lateral condyle of tibia

Medial condyle of tibia

Impression for iliotibial tract

Tuberosity of tibia

Medial border

Interosseous border

Medial surface

Anterior border

Medial malleolus

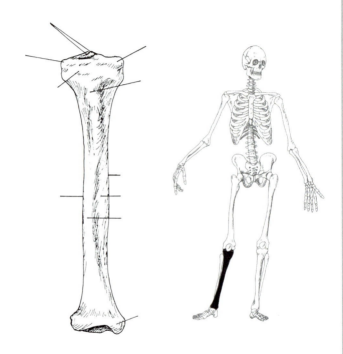

Tibia

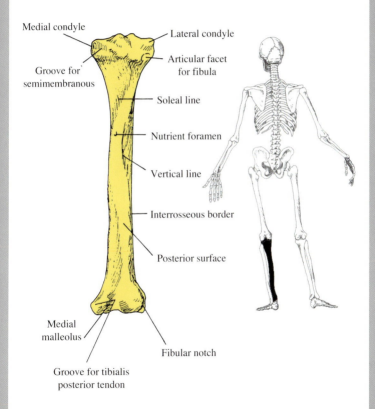

Medial condyle

Lateral condyle

Articular facet for fibula

Groove for semimembranous

Soleal line

Nutrient foramen

Vertical line

Interrosseous border

Posterior surface

Medial malleolus

Fibular notch

Groove for tibialis posterior tendon

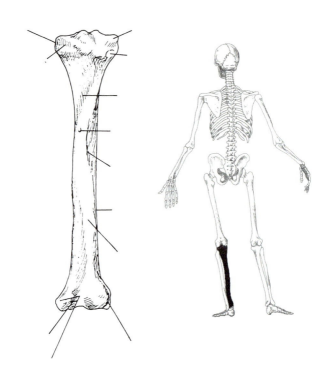

Fibula

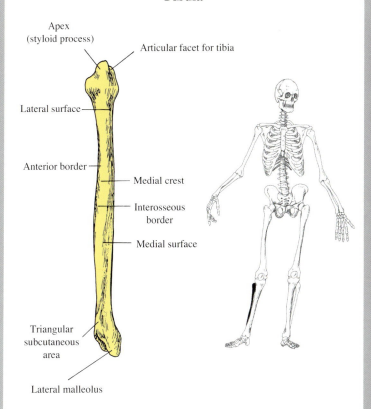

Apex
(styloid process)

Articular facet for tibia

Lateral surface

Anterior border

Medial crest

Interosseous
border

Medial surface

Triangular
subcutaneous
area

Lateral malleolus

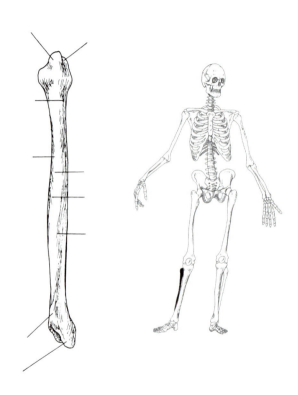

Fibula

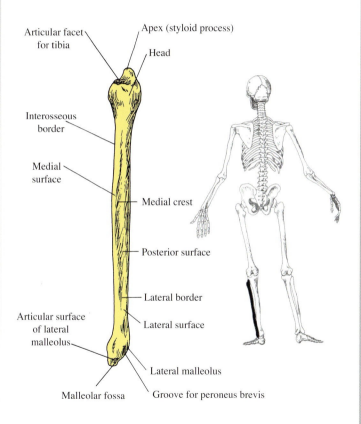

Apex (styloid process)

Articular facet for tibia

Head

Interosseous border

Medial surface

Medial crest

Posterior surface

Lateral border

Lateral surface

Articular surface of lateral malleolus

Lateral malleolus

Malleolar fossa

Groove for peroneus brevis

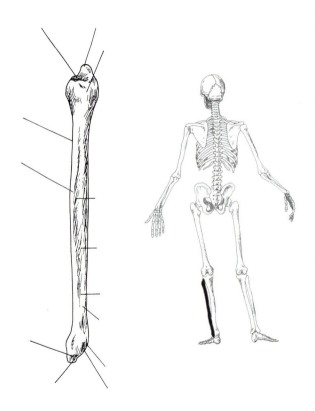

Tarsus, Metatarsus and Phalanges

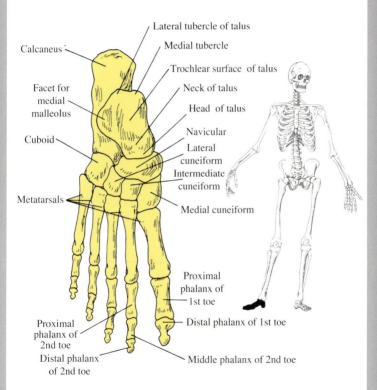

Lateral tubercle of talus

Medial tubercle

Calcaneus

Trochlear surface of talus

Facet for medial malleolus

Neck of talus

Head of talus

Navicular

Cuboid

Lateral cuneiform

Intermediate cuneiform

Metatarsals

Medial cuneiform

Proximal phalanx of 1st toe

Distal phalanx of 1st toe

Proximal phalanx of 2nd toe

Distal phalanx of 2nd toe

Middle phalanx of 2nd toe

View: Dorsal

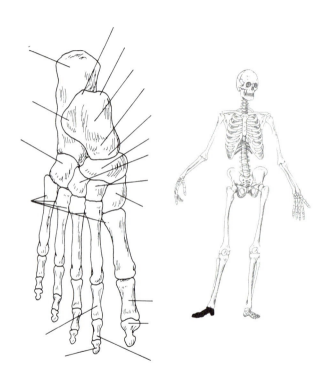

Tarsus, Metatarsus and Phalanges

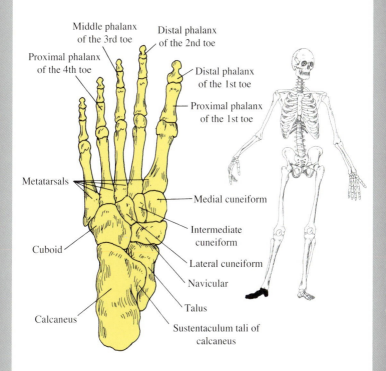

Middle phalanx
of the 3rd toe

Distal phalanx
of the 2nd toe

Proximal phalanx
of the 4th toe

Distal phalanx
of the 1st toe

Proximal phalanx
of the 1st toe

Metatarsals

Medial cuneiform

Intermediate
cuneiform

Cuboid

Lateral cuneiform

Navicular

Talus

Calcaneus

Sustentaculum tali of
calcaneus

View: Plantar

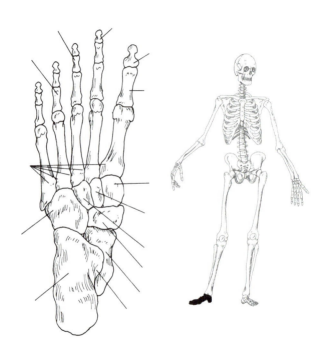

Talus

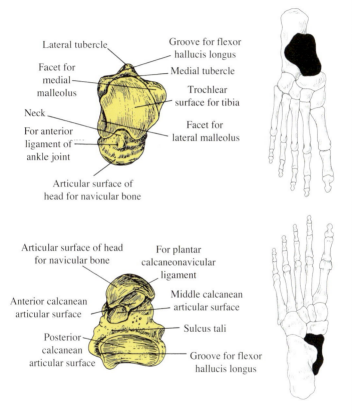

Lateral tubercle

Facet for medial malleolus

Neck

For anterior ligament of ankle joint

Articular surface of head for navicular bone

Groove for flexor hallucis longus

Medial tubercle

Trochlear surface for tibia

Facet for lateral malleolus

Articular surface of head for navicular bone

For plantar calcaneonavicular ligament

Anterior calcanean articular surface

Posterior calcanean articular surface

Middle calcanean articular surface

Sulcus tali

Groove for flexor hallucis longus

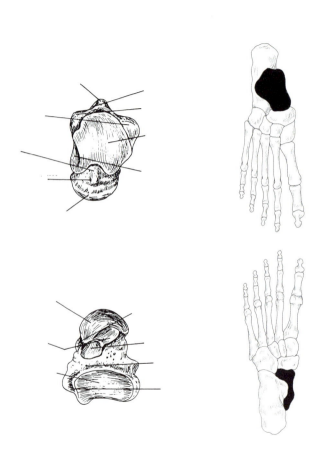

Talus

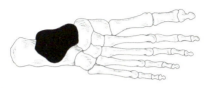

View: *Lateral*

Trochlear surface for tibia

Facet for lateral malleolus

Neck

For anterior ligament of ankle joint

Articular surface of head for navicular bone

Sulcus tali

Posterior calcanean facet on plantar surface

Lateral process

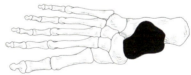

Facet for medial malleolus

Neck

Trochlear surface for tibia

For anterior ligament of ankle joint

View: *Medial*

Articular surface of head for navicular bone

For deltoid ligament

Lateral tubercle

Medial tubercle

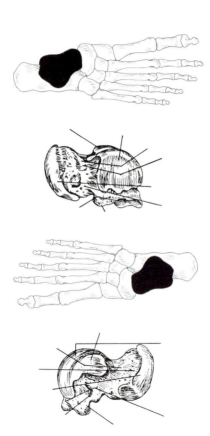

Calcaneus

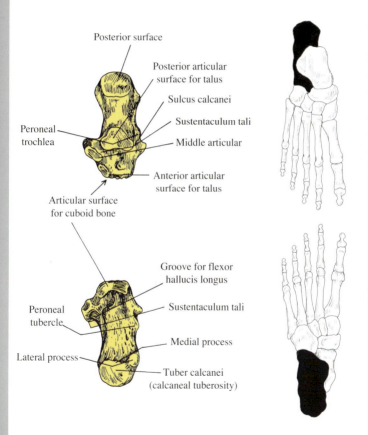

Posterior surface

Posterior articular surface for talus

Sulcus calcanei

Sustentaculum tali

Middle articular

Peroneal trochlea

Anterior articular surface for talus

Articular surface for cuboid bone

Groove for flexor hallucis longus

Sustentaculum tali

Peroneal tubercle

Medial process

Lateral process

Tuber calcanei (calcaneal tuberosity)

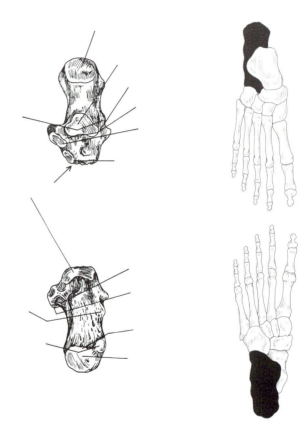

Calcaneus

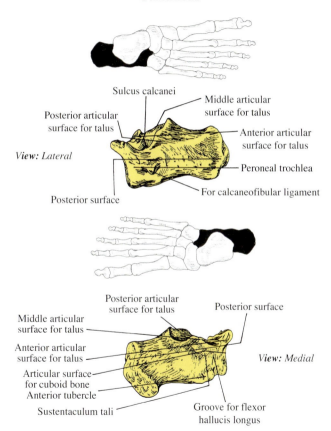

Sulcus calcanei

Middle articular surface for talus

Posterior articular surface for talus

Anterior articular surface for talus

View: Lateral

Peroneal trochlea

Posterior surface

For calcaneofibular ligament

Posterior articular surface for talus

Posterior surface

Middle articular surface for talus

Anterior articular surface for talus

View: Medial

Articular surface for cuboid bone

Anterior tubercle

Sustentaculum tali

Groove for flexor hallucis longus

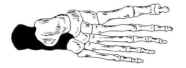

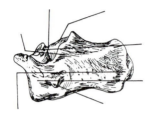

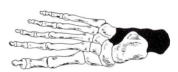

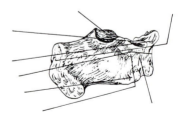

Navicular

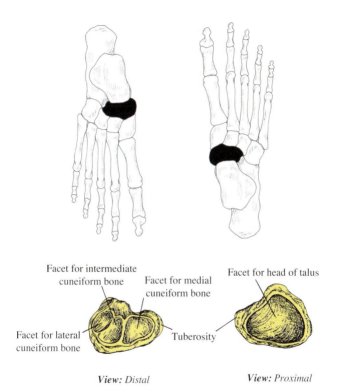

Facet for intermediate cuneiform bone

Facet for medial cuneiform bone

Facet for lateral cuneiform bone

Tuberosity

Facet for head of talus

View: Distal

View: Proximal

Note: The lateral surface can often bear a facet for articulation with the cuboid.

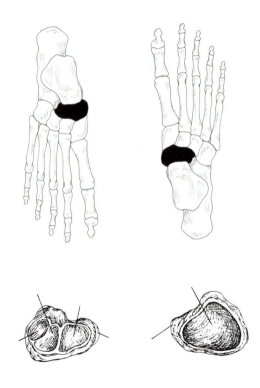

Cuboid

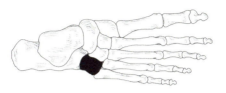

View: *Medial*

Facet for lateral
cuneiform bone

Occasional facet
for navicular bone

Facet for 4th
metatarsal bone

Facet for calcaneus

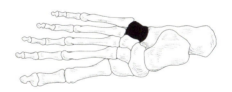

View: *Lateral*

Dorsal surface

Lateral surface

Facet for calcaneus

Facet for 4th metatarsal

Facet for 5th metatarsal

Facet on tuberosity for
sesamoid bone in
peroneus longus tendon

Groove for peroneus
longus tendon

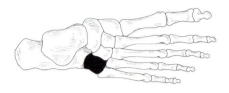

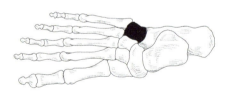

Medial Cuneiform

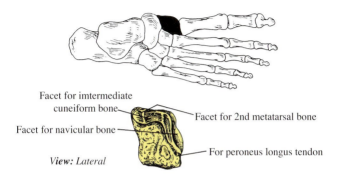

Facet for imtermediate cuneiform bone

Facet for navicular bone

Facet for 2nd metatarsal bone

For peroneus longus tendon

View: Lateral

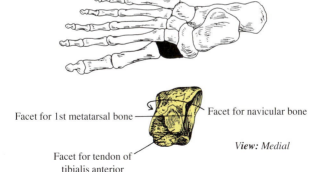

Facet for 1st metatarsal bone

Facet for navicular bone

Facet for tendon of tibialis anterior

View: Medial

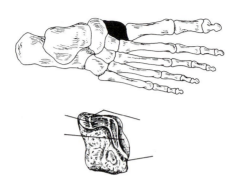

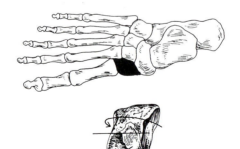

Intermediate Cuneiform

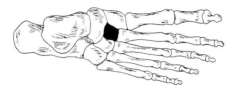

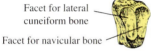

Facet for lateral
cuneiform bone

Facet for navicular bone

View: Proximal lateral

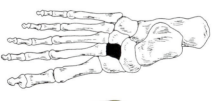

Facet for 2nd
metatarsal bone

Facet for medial
cuneiform bone

View: Distal medial

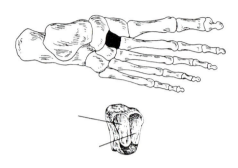

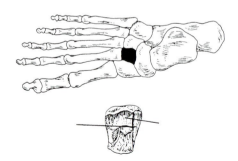

Licking Cuneiform

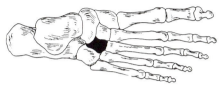

Facet for 4th metatarsal bone

Facet for cuboid bone

Facet for 3rd metatarsal bone

View: *Lateral*

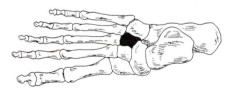

Facet for intermediate cuneiform bone

Facet for 2nd metatarsal bone

Facet for navicular bone

View: *Medial*

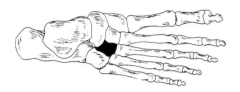

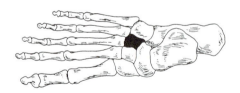

First Metatarsal

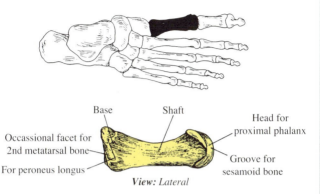

Base Shaft

Head for
proximal phalanx

Occassional facet for
2nd metatarsal bone

Groove for
sesamoid bone

For peroneus longus

View: *Lateral*

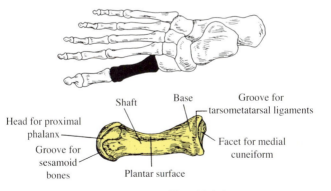

Shaft Base

Groove for
tarsometatarsal ligaments

Head for proximal
phalanx

Facet for medial
cuneiform

Groove for
sesamoid
bones

Plantar surface

View: *Medial*

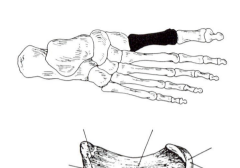

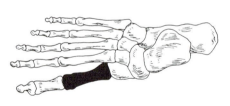

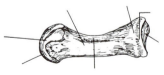

Second Metatarsal

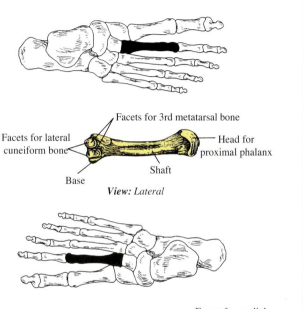

Facets for 3rd metatarsal bone

Facets for lateral
cuneiform bone

Head for
proximal phalanx

Shaft

Base

View: *Lateral*

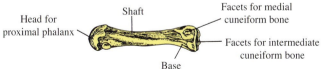

Shaft

Facets for medial
cuneiform bone

Head for
proximal phalanx

Facets for intermediate
cuneiform bone

Base

View: *Medial*

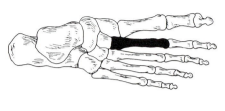

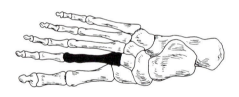

Third Metatarsal

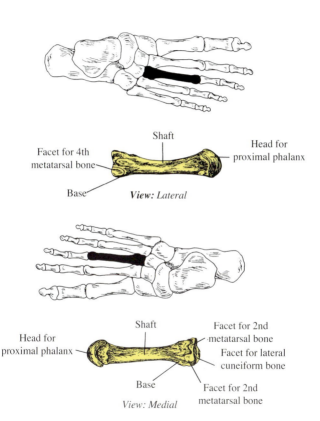

Facet for 4th
metatarsal bone

Shaft

Head for
proximal phalanx

Base

View: *Lateral*

Shaft

Head for
proximal phalanx

Facet for 2nd
metatarsal bone

Facet for lateral
cuneiform bone

Base

Facet for 2nd
metatarsal bone

View: Medial

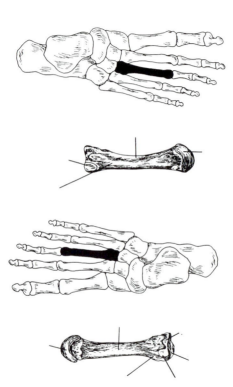

Fourth Metatarsal

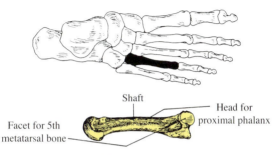

Shaft

Head for
proximal phalanx

Facet for 5th
metatarsal bone

View: *Lateral*

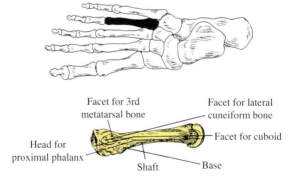

Facet for 3rd
metatarsal bone

Facet for lateral
cuneiform bone

Facet for cuboid

Head for
proximal phalanx

Shaft

Base

View: *Medial*

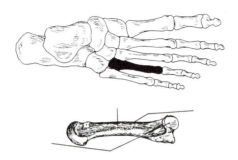

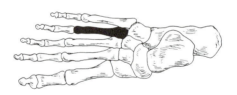

Fifth Metatarsal

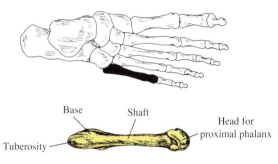

Base   Shaft

Tuberosity

Head for
proximal phalanx

View: *Lateral*

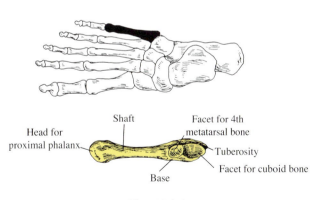

Shaft   Facet for 4th
metatarsal bone

Head for
proximal phalanx

Tuberosity

Facet for cuboid bone

Base

View: *Medial*

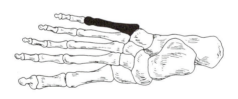

Joints and Ligaments

Continued overleaf........

Joints and Ligaments

continued...

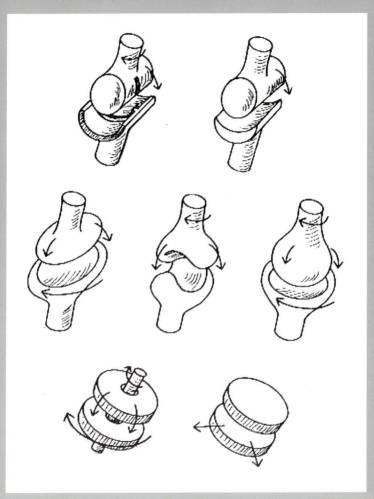

2

Temporomandibular Joint

Innervation: Auriculotemporal and masseteric branches of the mandibular division of the trigeminal nerve.

Arteries: Superficial temporal and maxillary arteries.

Movements: Depression, elevation, protrusion, retraction, and lateral movements.

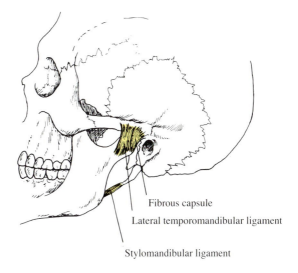

Fibrous capsule

Lateral temporomandibular ligament

Stylomandibular ligament

View: *Left lateral*

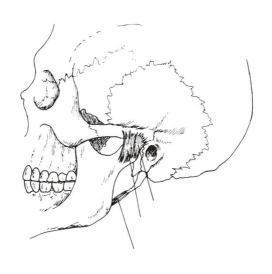

Temporomandibular Joint

Innervation: Auriculotemporal and masseteric branches of the mandibular division of the trigeminal nerve.

Arteries: Superficial temporal and maxillary arteries.

Movements: Depression, elevation, protrusion, retraction, and lateral movements.

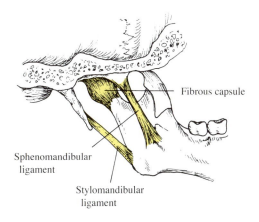

Fibrous capsule

Sphenomandibular ligament

Stylomandibular ligament

View: *Left medial*

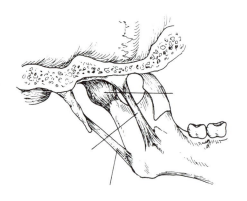

Temporomandibular Joint

Innervation: Auriculotemporal and masseteric branches of the mandibular division of the trigeminal nerve.

Arteries: Superficial temporal and maxillary arteries.

Movements: Depression, elevation, protrusion, retraction, and lateral movements.

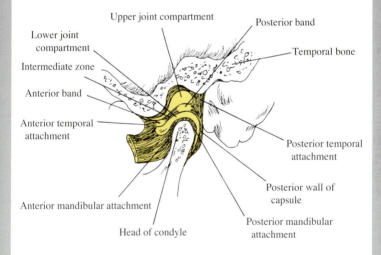

View: *Left lateral*

Sagittal Section

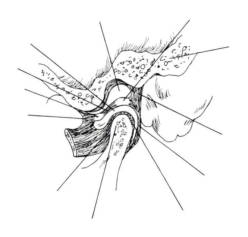

Temporomandibular Joint

Innervation: Auriculotemporal and masseteric branches of the mandibular division of the trigeminal nerve.

Arteries: Superficial temporal and maxillary arteries.

Movements: Depression, elevation, protrusion, retraction, and lateral movements.

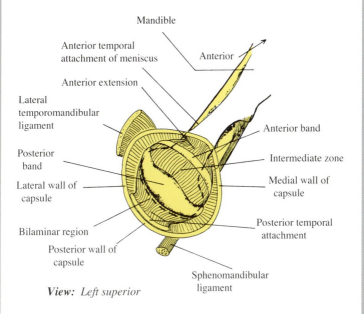

Mandible

Anterior temporal attachment of meniscus

Anterior

Anterior extension

Lateral temporomandibular ligament

Anterior band

Posterior band

Intermediate zone

Lateral wall of capsule

Medial wall of capsule

Bilaminar region

Posterior temporal attachment

Posterior wall of capsule

Sphenomandibular ligament

View: Left superior

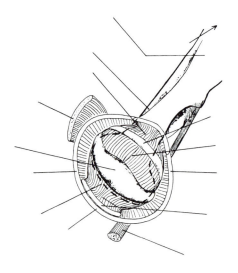

Craniovertebral Joints
Atlanto-occipital and Atlanto-axial Joints

Innervation: Medial branches of the dorsal rami and recurrent meningeal branches of the ventral rami of adjacent spinal nerves.

Arteries: Spinal branches of the vertebral arteries.

Movements: Flexion, extension, lateral flexion, rotation and circumduction.

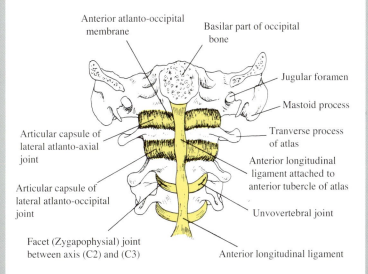

Anterior atlanto-occipital membrane

Basilar part of occipital bone

Jugular foramen

Mastoid process

Articular capsule of lateral atlanto-axial joint

Tranverse process of atlas

Anterior longitudinal ligament attached to anterior tubercle of atlas

Articular capsule of lateral atlanto-occipital joint

Unvovertebral joint

Facet (Zygapophysial) joint between axis (C2) and (C3)

Anterior longitudinal ligament

View: Anterior

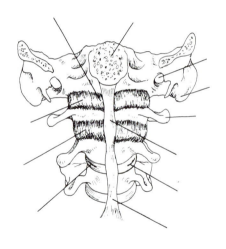

Craniovertebral Joints
Atlanto-occipital and Atlanto-axial Joints

Innervation: Medial branches of the dorsal rami and recurrent meningeal branches of the ventral rami of adjacent spinal nerves.

Arteries: Spinal branches of the vertebral arteries.

Movements: Flexion, extension, lateral flexion, rotation and circumduction.

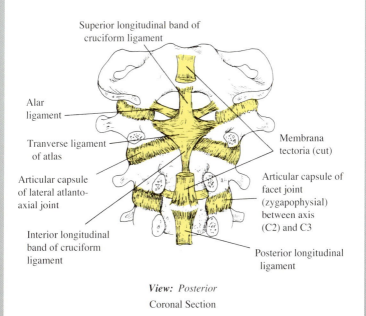

Superior longitudinal band of cruciform ligament

Alar ligament

Tranverse ligament of atlas

Articular capsule of lateral atlanto-axial joint

Interior longitudinal band of cruciform ligament

Membrana tectoria (cut)

Articular capsule of facet joint (zygapophysial) between axis (C2) and C3

Posterior longitudinal ligament

View: Posterior
Coronal Section

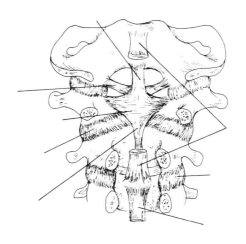

Craniovertebral Joints
Atlanto-occipital and Atlanto-axial Joints

Innervation: Medial branches of the dorsal rami and recurrent menigeal branches of the ventral rami of adjacent spinal nerves.

Arteries: Spinal branches of the vertebral arteries.

Movements: Flexion, extension, lateral flexion, rotation and circumduction.

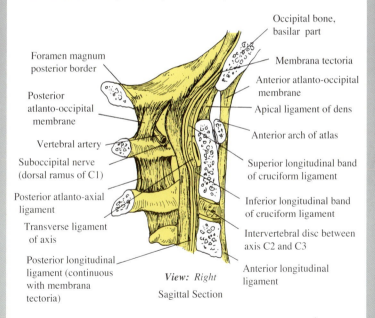

Occipital bone, basilar part

Membrana tectoria

Anterior atlanto-occipital membrane

Apical ligament of dens

Anterior arch of atlas

Superior longitudinal band of cruciform ligament

Inferior longitudinal band of cruciform ligament

Intervertebral disc between axis C2 and C3

Anterior longitudinal ligament

Foramen magnum posterior border

Posterior atlanto-occipital membrane

Vertebral artery

Suboccipital nerve (dorsal ramus of C1)

Posterior atlanto-axial ligament

Transverse ligament of axis

Posterior longitudinal ligament (continuous with membrana tectoria)

View: Right
Sagittal Section

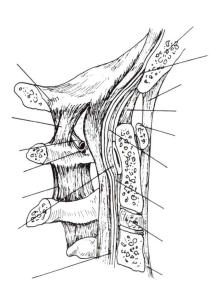

Median Atlanto-Axial Joint

Innervation: Medial branches of the dorsal rami and recurrent meningeal branches of the ventral rami of adjacent spinal nerves.

Arteries: Spinal branches of the vertebral arteries.

Movements: Flexion, extension, lateral flexion, rotation, and circumduction.

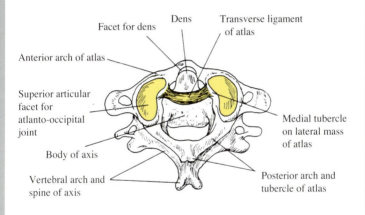

View: Superior, posterior

Note: There are 3 atlanto-axial joints: 2 lateral and one median. See also cards 116 and 117.

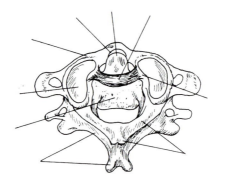

Joints of Vertebral Bodies

Innervation: Medial branches of the dorsal rami and recurrent meningeal branches of the ventral rami of adjacent spinal nerves.

Arteries: Spinal branches of the vertebral arteries.

Movements: Flexion, extension, lateral flexion, rotation and circumduction.

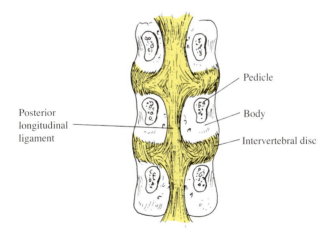

Pedicle

Body

Posterior longitudinal ligament

Intervertebral disc

View:* *Posterior
Coronal Section

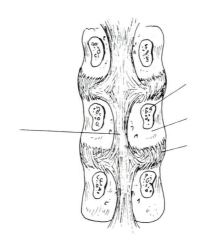

Joints of Vertebral Bodies and Arches of Lumbar Vertebrae

Innervation: Medial branches of the dorsal rami and recurrent meningeal branches of the ventral rami of adjacent spinal nerves.

Arteries: Spinal branches of the lumbar arteries.

Movements: Flexion, extension, lateral flexion, rotation and circumduction.

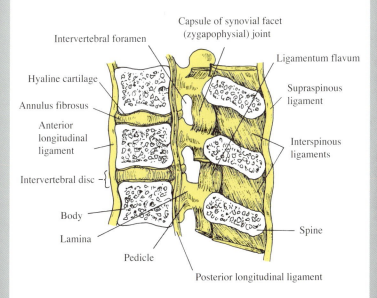

View: Right lateral

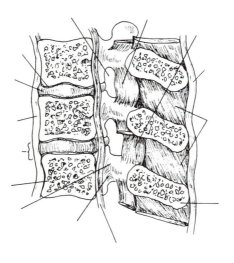

Joints of Vertebral Arches
of Lumbar Vertebrae

Innervation: Medial branches of the dorsal rami and recurrent meningeal branches of the ventral rami of adjacent spinal nerve.

Arteries: Spinal branches of the lumbar arteries.

Movements: Flexion, extension, lateral flexion, rotation and circumduction

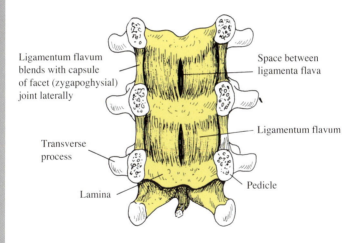

Ligamentum flavum blends with capsule of facet (zygapoghysial) joint laterally

Space between ligamenta flava

Ligamentum flavum

Transverse process

Pedicle

Lamina

View: Anterior
Coronal Section

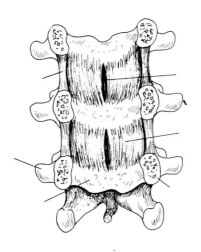

Costovertebral Joints

Innervation: Intercostal nerves.

Arteries: Spinal branches of the posterior intercostal arteries.

Movements: During inspiration slight gliding. Movements at these joints guided by the shape and direction of the articular surfaces produce evelation (pump handle movement) of the upper six ribs and eversion (bucket handle movement) of the lower six ribs.

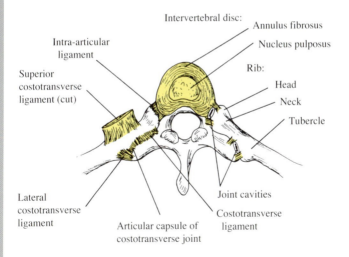

Intervertebral disc:
Annulus fibrosus
Nucleus pulposus

Intra-articular ligament

Superior costotransverse ligament (cut)

Rib:
Head
Neck
Tubercle

Lateral costotransverse ligament

Joint cavities

Articular capsule of costotransverse joint

Costotransverse ligament

View: Superior

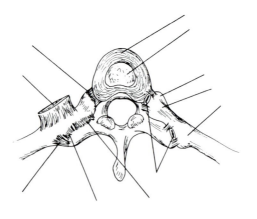

Costovertebral Joints

Innervation: Intercostal nerves.

Arteries: Spinal Branches of the posterior intercostal arteries.

Movements: During inspiration slight gliding. Movements at these joints guided by the shape and direction of the articular surfaces produce evelation (pump handle movement) of the upper six ribs and eversion (bucket handle movements) of the lower six ribs.

Superior costal demifacet for head of rib

Facet on tranverse process for tubercle of rib

Body

Radiate ligament

Superior costo-tranverse ligaments

Anterior longitudinal ligament

Intervertebral disc

Paired synovial joints

Intra-articular ligament

Rib shaft

Rib head

View: Right, anterolateral

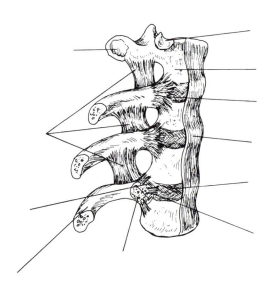

Sternocostal Joints

Innervation: Anterior cutaneous branches of the intercostal nerves.

Arteries: Branches from the internal thoracic artery.

Movements: Slight gliding sufficient for respiration.

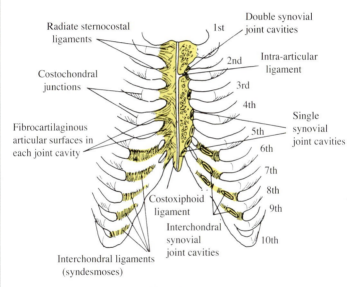

Radiate sternocostal ligaments

Costochondral junctions

Fibrocartilaginous articular surfaces in each joint cavity

1st

2nd

3rd

4th

5th

6th

7th

8th

9th

10th

Double synovial joint cavities

Intra-articular ligament

Single synovial joint cavities

Costoxiphoid ligament

Interchondral synovial joint cavities

Interchondral ligaments (syndesmoses)

View: Anterior

Note: The synarthrosis joint of the first rib and the synovial cavities of the second to seventh are exposed by a coronal section of the sternum and costal cartilages.

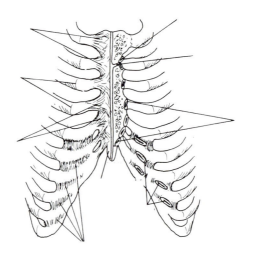

Sternoclavicular Joints

Innervation: Anterior supraclavicular and the nerve to the subclavius.

Arteries: Branches from the internal thoracic and suprascapular arteries.

Movements: (As assoicated with those of the scapula). Elevation, depression, protraction, retraction, upward and downward rotation.

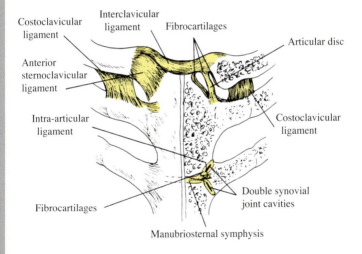

Costoclavicular ligament

Interclavicular ligament

Fibrocartilages

Articular disc

Anterior sternoclavicular ligament

Intra-articular ligament

Costoclavicular ligament

Fibrocartilages

Double synovial joint cavities

Manubriosternal symphysis

View: *Anterior*

Note: Right joint is intact and left is in a coronal section

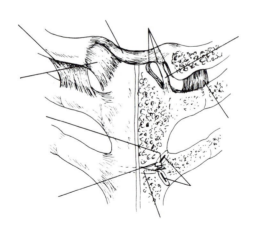

Acromioclavicular Joints

Innervation: Suprascapular and lateral pectoral nerves.

Arteries: Suprascapular and thoraco-acrominal arteries.

Movements: (As associated with those of the scapula.) Elevation, depression, protraction, retraction, upward and downward rotation.

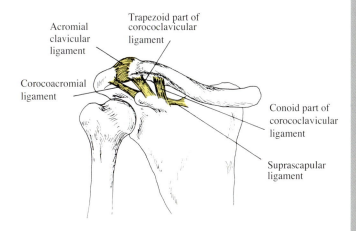

Acromial clavicular ligament

Trapezoid part of corococlavicular ligament

Corocoacromial ligament

Conoid part of corococlavicular ligament

Suprascapular ligament

View: *Anterior inferior*

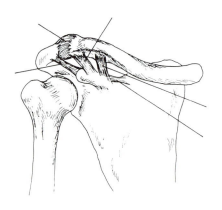

Glenohumeral Joint
(Shoulder Joint)

Innervation: Posterior cord of the brachial plexus and the suprascapular axillar lateral pectoral nerves.

Arteries: Anterior and posterior circumflex humeral and suprascapular arteries.

Movements: Flexion - extension, abduction - adduction, circumduction, medial, and lateral rotation.

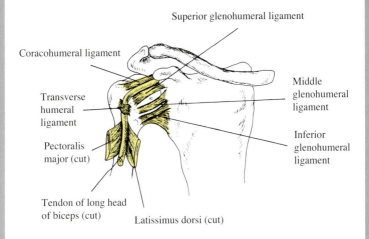

Superior glenohumeral ligament

Coracohumeral ligament

Transverse humeral ligament

Pectoralis major (cut)

Tendon of long head of biceps (cut)

Latissimus dorsi (cut)

Middle glenohumeral ligament

Inferior glenohumeral ligament

View: *Anterior inferior*

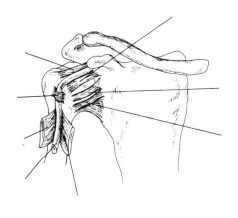

Glenohumeral Joint
(Shoulder Joint)

Innervation: Posterior cord of the brachial plexus and the suprascapular, axillar lateral pectoral nerves.

Arteries: Anterior and posterior circumflex humeral and suprascapular arteries.

Movements: Flexion - extension, abduction - adduction, circumduction, medial, and lateral rotation.

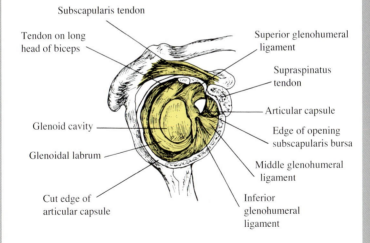

Subscapularis tendon

Tendon on long head of biceps

Superior glenohumeral ligament

Supraspinatus tendon

Glenoid cavity

Articular capsule

Edge of opening subscapularis bursa

Glenoidal labrum

Middle glenohumeral ligament

Cut edge of articular capsule

Inferior glenohumeral ligament

View: *Anterolateral with head of humerus removed.*

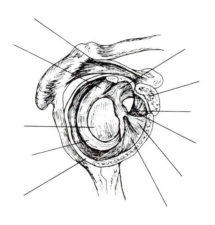

Elbow and Proximal Radio-Ulnar Joints

Innervation: Mostly musculocutaneous and radial nerves with contributions from ulnar, median and sometimes anterior interosseous nerves.

Arteries: Anastomotic network around the elbow fomed by branches of profunda brachii, brachial, radial, and ulnar arteries.

Movements: Flexion and extension at the elbow joint. Supination and pronation at the proximal radio-ulnar joint.

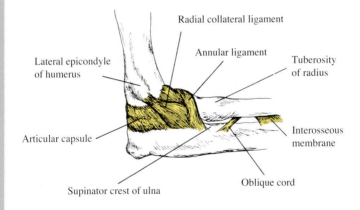

Radial collateral ligament

Annular ligament

Lateral epicondyle of humerus

Tuberosity of radius

Interosseous membrane

Articular capsule

Supinator crest of ulna

Oblique cord

View: *Lateral*

Note: The forearm is flexed at the elbow 90 degrees and is completely supinated.

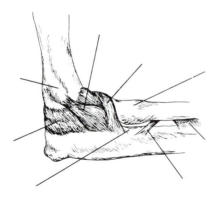

Elbow and Proximal Radio-Ulnar Joints

Innervation: Mostly musculocutaneous and radial nerves with contributions from ulnar, median and sometimes anterior interosseous nerves.

Arteries: Anastomotic network around the elbow formed by branches of profunda brachii, brachial, radial and ulnar arteries.

Movements: Flexion and extension at the elbow joint. Supination and pronation at the proximal radio-ulnar joint.

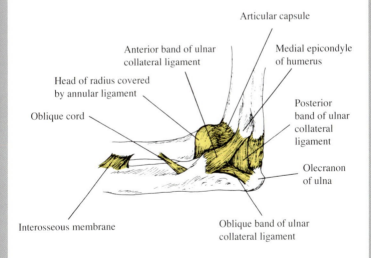

View: Medial

Note: The forearm is flexed at the elbow 90 degrees and is semi-supinated.

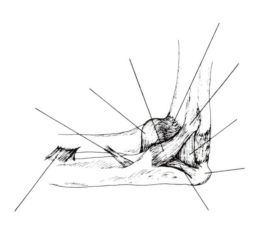

Radio-Ulnar Joints

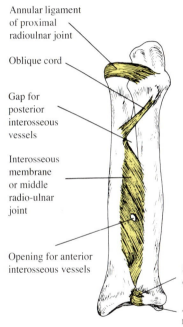

Annular ligament of proximal radioulnar joint

Oblique cord

Gap for posterior interosseous vessels

Interosseous membrane or middle radio-ulnar joint

Opening for anterior interosseous vessels

Sacciform recess of capsule of distal radio-ulnar joint

Articular disc of distal radio-ulnar joint

Innervation: Anterior interosseous branch of median nerve and posterior interosseous branch of radial nerve.

Arteries: Anterior interosseous artery.

Movements: Pronation and supination.

View: Anterior

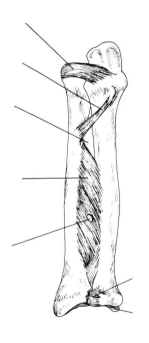

Radiocarpal Joint
(Wrist Joint)

Innervation: Anterior and posterior interosseous nerves.

Arteries: Anterior interosseous artery, anterior and posterior carpal branches of radial and ulnar arteries, palmar and dorsal metacarpal arteries and recurrent branches of deep palmar arch.

Movements: Flexion, extension, ulnar and radial deviation and circumduction.

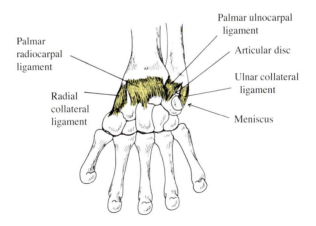

Palmar ulnocarpal ligament

Articular disc

Ulnar collateral ligament

Meniscus

Palmar radiocarpal ligament

Radial collateral ligament

View: Palmar

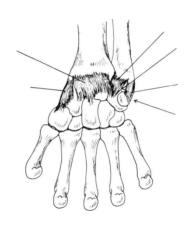

Radiocarpal Joint
(Wrist Joints)

Innervation: Anterior and posterior interosseous nerves.

Arteries: Anterior interosseous artery, anterior and posterior carpal branches of radial and ulnar arteries, palmar and dorsal metacarpal arteries and recurrent branches of deep palmar arch.

Movements: Flexion, extension, ulnar and radial deviation, and circumduction.

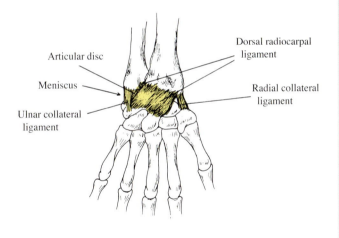

Articular disc

Meniscus

Ulnar collateral ligament

Dorsal radiocarpal ligament

Radial collateral ligament

View: Dorsal

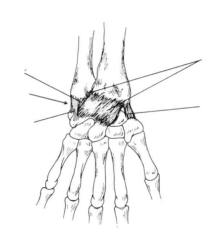

Intercarpal Joints

Innervation: Anterior and posterior interosseous nerves.

Arteries: Anterior interosseous artery, anterior and posterior carpal branches of radial and ulnar arteries, palmar and dorsal metacarpal arteries and recurrent branches of deep palmar arch.

Movements: Slight gliding at the intercarpal joints, increases the range of movements at the wrist joint. Flexion - extension, ulnar - radial deviation and circumduction.

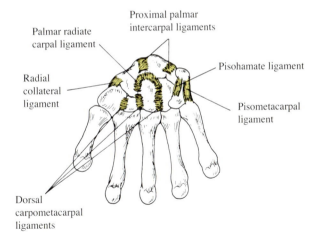

Proximal palmar intercarpal ligaments

Palmar radiate carpal ligament

Pisohamate ligament

Radial collateral ligament

Pisometacarpal ligament

Dorsal carpometacarpal ligaments

View: Palmar

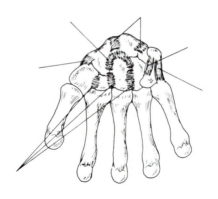

Intercarpal Joints

Innervation: Anterior and posterior interosseous nerves.

Arteries: Anterior interosseous artery, anterior and posterior carpal branches of radial and ulnar arteries, palmar and dorsal metacarpal arteries and recurrent branches of deep palmar arch.

Movements: Slight gliding at the intercarpal joints, increases the range of movements at the wrist joint. Flexion - extension, ulnar - radial deviation, and circumduction.

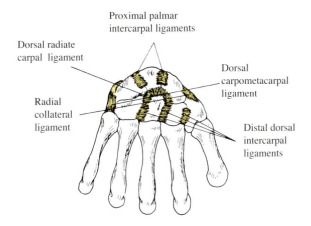

Proximal palmar intercarpal ligaments

Dorsal radiate carpal ligament

Radial collateral ligament

Dorsal carpometacarpal ligament

Distal dorsal intercarpal ligaments

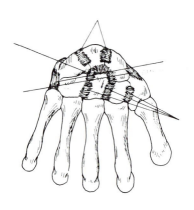

Carpometacarpal and Intercarpal Joints

Innervation: Anterior and posterior interosseous nerves.

Arteries: Anterior interosseous artery, anterior and posterior carpal branches of radial and ulnar arteries, palmar and dorsal metacarpal arteries and recurrent branches of deep palmar arch.

Movement: (For the fingers) Slight gliding which allows flexion - extension and adjunct rotation.
(For the thumb) Flexion - extension combined with conjunct medial - lateral rotation, abduction - adduction, opposition and circumduction.

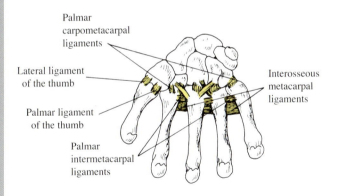

Palmar carpometacarpal ligaments

Lateral ligament of the thumb

Palmar ligament of the thumb

Palmar intermetacarpal ligaments

Interosseous metacarpal ligaments

View: *Palmar*

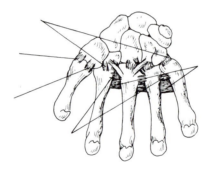

Carpometacarpal and Intercarpal Joints

Innervation: Anterior and posterior interosseous nerves.

Arteries: Anterior interosseous artery, anterior and posterior carpal branches of radial and ulnar arteries, palmar and dorsal metacarpal arteries and recurrent branches of deep palmar arch.

Movement: (For the fingers) Slight gliding which allows flexion - extension and adjunct rotation.
(For the thumb) Flexion - extension combined with conjunct medial - lateral rotation, abduction - adduction, opposition and circumduction.

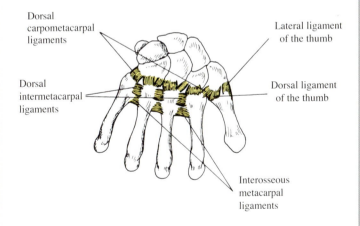

Dorsal carpometacarpal ligaments

Lateral ligament of the thumb

Dorsal intermetacarpal ligaments

Dorsal ligament of the thumb

Interosseous metacarpal ligaments

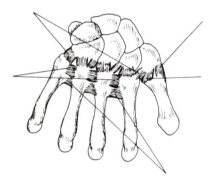

Metacarpophalangeal and Interphalangeal Joints

Innervation: Palmar digital branches of median (radial 3 1/2 digits) and ulnar (ulnar 1 1/2 digits) nerves.

Arteries: Princeps pollicis, radialis indicis, and palmar and dorsal digital arteries.

Movements: Metacarpophalangeal joints: Flexion - extension combined with conjunct rotation, abduction - adduction and circumduction.

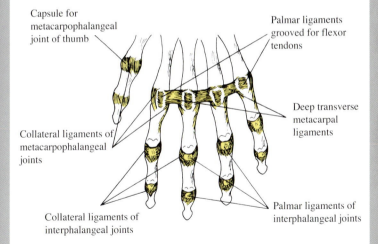

Capsule for metacarpophalangeal joint of thumb

Palmar ligaments grooved for flexor tendons

Deep transverse metacarpal ligaments

Collateral ligaments of metacarpophalangeal joints

Collateral ligaments of interphalangeal joints

Palmar ligaments of interphalangeal joints

View: Palmar

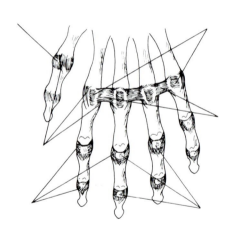

Pubic Symphysis
(Coronal Section)

Innervation: Pudendal nerve.

Arteries: Internal pudendal artery.

Movements: Slight angulation, rotation and displacement are possible. Further slight separation may occur in late gestation and during child birth.

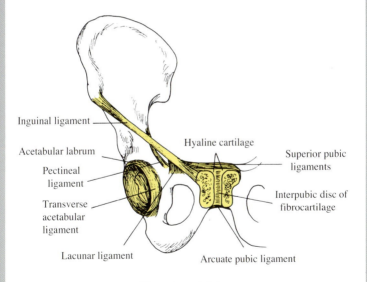

Inguinal ligament

Acetabular labrum

Pectineal ligament

Transverse acetabular ligament

Lacunar ligament

Hyaline cartilage

Superior pubic ligaments

Interpubic disc of fibrocartilage

Arcuate pubic ligament

View: Anteroinferior

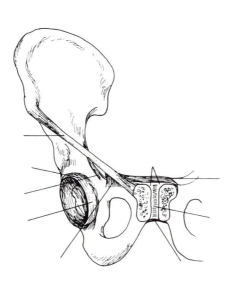

Lumbosacral, Sacrococcygeal and Sacro-iliac Joints

Innervation: Superior gluteal nerve, sacral plexus, and the dorsal rami of S1 and S2 spinal nerves.

Arteries: Superior gluteal, iliolumbar and lateral sacral arteries.

Movements: For sacro-iliac joint; slight anteroposterior rotation around a transverse axis.

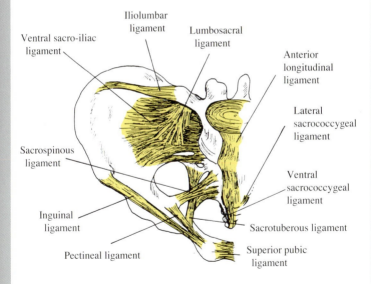

Iliolumbar ligament

Lumbosacral ligament

Ventral sacro-iliac ligament

Anterior longitudinal ligament

Lateral sacrococcygeal ligament

Sacrospinous ligament

Ventral sacrococcygeal ligament

Inguinal ligament

Pectineal ligament

Sacrotuberous ligament

Superior pubic ligament

View: Anterosuperior

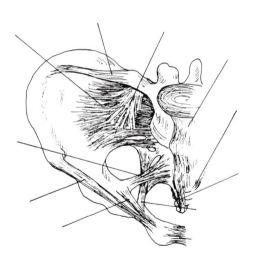

Lumbosacral, Sacrococcygeal and Sacro-iliac Joints

Innervation: Superior gluteal nerve, sacral plexus, and the dorsal rami of S1 and S2 spinal nerves.

Arteries: Superior gluteal, iliolumbar and lateral sacral arteries.

Movement: For sacro-iliac joint; slight anteroposterior rotation around a transverse axis.

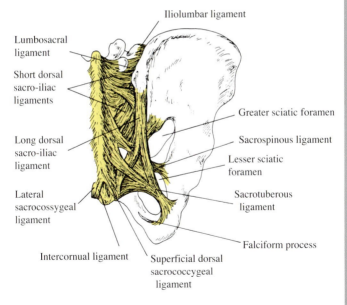

Iliolumbar ligament

Lumbosacral ligament

Short dorsal sacro-iliac ligaments

Long dorsal sacro-iliac ligament

Lateral sacrococsygeal ligament

Greater sciatic foramen

Sacrospinous ligament

Lesser sciatic foramen

Sacrotuberous ligament

Falciform process

Intercornual ligament

Superficial dorsal sacrococcygeal ligament

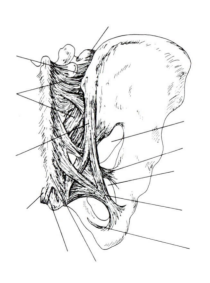

Hip (Coxal) Joint

Innervation: Femoral, obturator, accessory obturator, the nerve to quadratus femoris and the superior gluteal nerves.

Arteries: Branches from the obturator, medial circumflex femoral, and superior and inferior gluteal arteries.

Movements: Flexion - extension, abduction - adduction, circumduction, medial and lateral rotation.

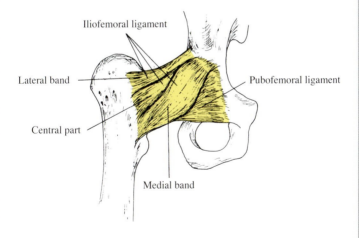

View: Anterior

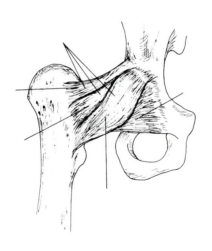

Hip (Coxal) Joint

Innervation: Femoral, obturator, accessory obturator, the nerve to quadratus femoris and the superior gluteal nerves.

Arteries: Branches from the obturator, medial circumflex femoral, and superior and inferior gluteal arteries.

Movement: Flexion - extension, abduction - adduction, circumduction, medial and lateral rotation.

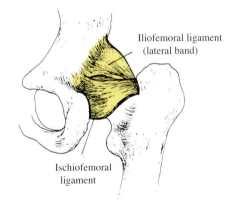

Iliofemoral ligament
(lateral band)

Ischiofemoral
ligament

View: *Posterior*

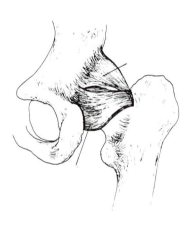

Hip (Coxal) Joint

Innervation: Femoral, obturator, accessory obturator, the nerve to quadratus femoris and the superior gluteal nerves.

Arteries: Branches from the obturator, medial circumflex femoral, and superior and inferior gluteal arteries.

Movement: Flexion - extension, abduction - adduction, circumduction, medial, and lateral rotation.

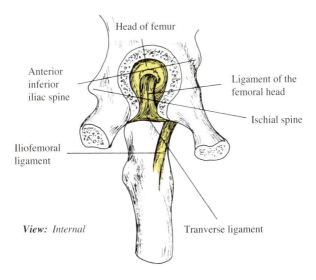

Head of femur

Anterior inferior iliac spine

Ligament of the femoral head

Ischial spine

Iliofemoral ligament

Tranverse ligament

View: Internal

Note: Right hip joint; the floor of the acetabulum is removed.

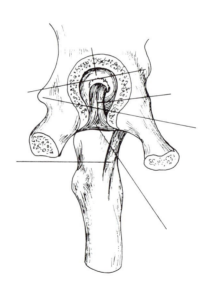

Knee Joint

Innervation: Obturator, femoral, tibial and common peroneal nerves.

Arteries: Descending genicular branches of the femoral, superior, middle, and inferior genicular branches of the popliteal, descending branch of the lateral circumflex femoral, and the anterior and posterior recurrent branches of the anterior tibial.

Movements: Flexion - extension, medial and lateral rotation.

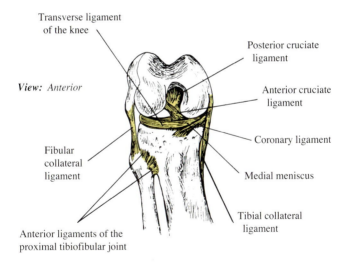

Transverse ligament of the knee

Posterior cruciate ligament

Anterior cruciate ligament

View: Anterior

Coronary ligament

Fibular collateral ligament

Medial meniscus

Tibial collateral ligament

Anterior ligaments of the proximal tibiofibular joint

Note: The right knee is in full flexion.

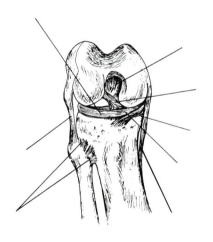

Knee Joint

Innervation: Obturator, femoral, tibial, and common peroneal nerves.

Arteries: Descending genicular branches of the femoral, superior, middle, and inferior genicular branches of the popliteal, descending branch of the lateral circumflex femoral, and the anterior and posterior recurrent branches of the anterior tibial.

Movements: Flexion - extension, medial and lateral rotation.

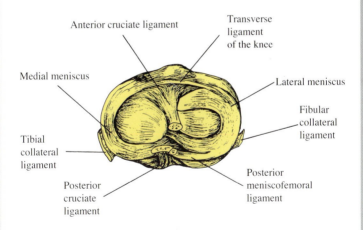

Anterior cruciate ligament

Transverse ligament of the knee

Medial meniscus

Lateral meniscus

Fibular collateral ligament

Tibial collateral ligament

Posterior cruciate ligament

Posterior meniscofemoral ligament

View: Superior

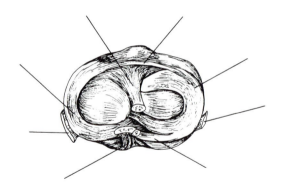

Knee Joint

Innervation: Obturator, femoral, tibial, and common peroneal nerves.

Arteries: Descending genicular branches of the femoral, superior, middle, and inferior genicular branches of the popliteal, descending branch of the lateral circumflex femoral, and the anterior and posterior recurrent branches of the anterior tibial.

Movements: Flexion - extension, medial and lateral rotation.

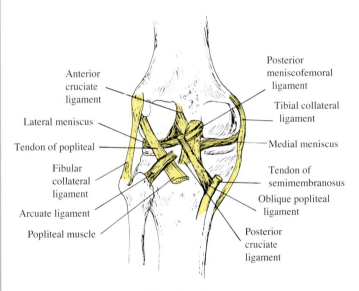

View: Posterior

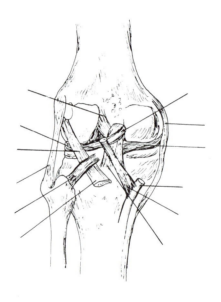

Knee Joint

Innervation: Obturator, femoral, tibial and common peroneal nerves.

Arteries: Descending genicular branches of the femoral, superior, middle, and inferior genicular branches of the popliteal, descending branch of the lateral circumflex femoral, and the anterior and posterior recurrent branches of the anterior tibial.

Movements: Flexion - extension, medial and lateral rotation.

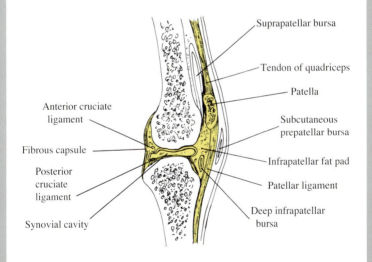

Sagittal Section

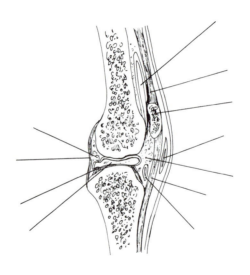

Tibiofibular Joints

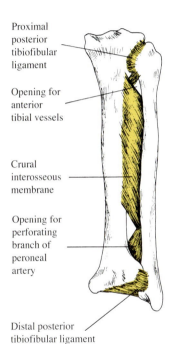

Proximal posterior tibiofibular ligament

Opening for anterior tibial vessels

Crural interosseous membrane

Opening for perforating branch of peroneal artery

Distal posterior tibiofibular ligament

Proximal Tibiofibular Joint:

Innervation: Common peroneal nerve and the nerve to the popliteus, (tibial nerve).

Arteries: Anterior and posterior tibial recurrent branches of the anterior tibial artery.

Movements: Slight lateral rotation of the fibula during dorsiflexion of the ankle.

Distal Tibiofibular Joint:

Innervation: Deep peroneal, tibial and saphenous nerves.

Arteries: Peroneal perforating branch and medial malleolar branches of the anterior and posterior tibial arteries.

Movements: Same as proximal joint.

View: Posterior

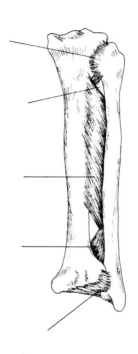

Talocrural or Ankle Joint

Innervation: Deep peroneal and tibial nerves.

Arteries: Malleolar branches of the anterior tibial and peroneal arteries.

Movements: Dorsiflexion and plantar flexion.

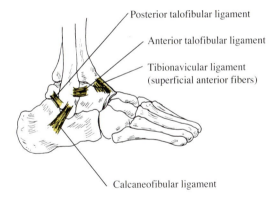

Posterior talofibular ligament

Anterior talofibular ligament

Tibionavicular ligament
(superficial anterior fibers)

Calcaneofibular ligament

View: *Anterolateral*

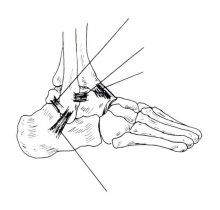

Talocrural or Ankle Joint

Innervation: Deep peroneal and tibial nerves.

Arteries: Malleolar branches of the anterior tibial and peroneal arteries.

Movements: Dorsiflexion and plantar flexion.

Parts of the deltoid ligament:

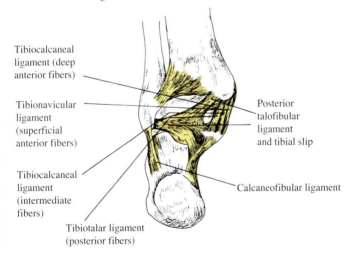

Tibiocalcaneal ligament (deep anterior fibers)

Tibionavicular ligament (superficial anterior fibers)

Tibiocalcaneal ligament (intermediate fibers)

Tibiotalar ligament (posterior fibers)

Posterior talofibular ligament and tibial slip

Calcaneofibular ligament

View: Posterior

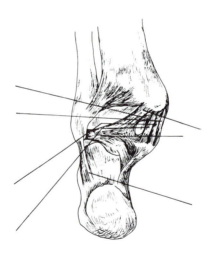

Talocrural or Ankle Joint

Innervation: Deep peroneal and tibial nerves.

Arteries: Malleolar branches of the anterior tibial and peroneal arteries.

Movements: Dorsiflexion and plantar flexion.

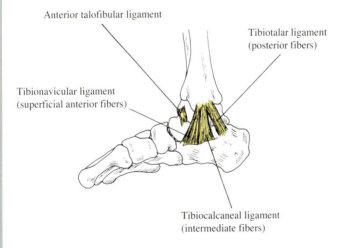

Anterior talofibular ligament

Tibiotalar ligament
(posterior fibers)

Tibionavicular ligament
(superficial anterior fibers)

Tibiocalcaneal ligament
(intermediate fibers)

View: Anteromedial

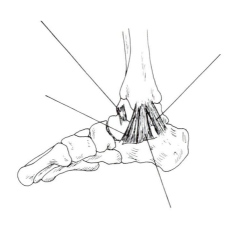

Subtalar, Intertarsal Joints
(Talocalcaneal, Talocalcaneonavicular and Calcaneocuboid Joints)

Innervation: Branches of the deep peroneal and medial and lateral plantar nerves.

Arteries: Anastomotic network around the ankle formed by branches of the anterior and posterior tibial, dorsalis pedis, peroneal, and medial and lateral plantar arteries.

Movements: Gliding and rotation at these joints produce inversion and eversion of the foot.

Interosseous talocalcaneal ligament

Cervical ligament

Talonavicular ligament

Subtalar joint

Bifurcated ligament:

Lateral talocalcaneal ligament

Long plantar ligament

Lateral calcaneonavicule ligament

Medial calcaneocuboid ligament

View: Anterolateral

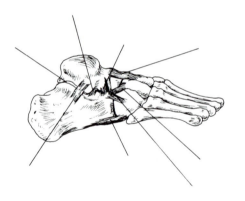

Subtalar, Intertarsal Joints
(Talocalcaneal, Talocalcaneonavicular and Calcaneocuboid Joints)

Innervation: Branches of the deep peroneal and medial and lateral plantar nerves.

Arteries: Anastomotic network around the ankle formed by branches of the anterior and posterior tibial, dorsalis pedis, peroneal, and medial and lateral plantar arteries.

Movements: Gliding and rotation at these joints produce inversion and eversion of the foot.

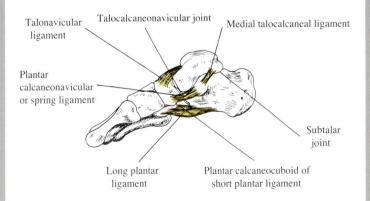

Talonavicular ligament

Talocalcaneonavicular joint

Medial talocalcaneal ligament

Plantar calcaneonavicular or spring ligament

Subtalar joint

Long plantar ligament

Plantar calcaneocuboid of short plantar ligament

View: *Anteromedial*

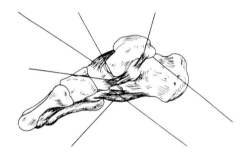

Intertarsal Joints
(Cuneonavicular, Cubideonavicular, Intercuneiform, and Cuneocuboid Joints)

Innervation: Branches of the deep peroneal and medial and lateral plantar nerves.

Arteries: Branches of the dorsalis pedis and medial and lateral plantar arteries.

Movements: Slight gliding and rotation at these joints contributes to inversion and eversion of the foot.

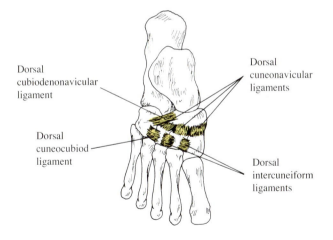

Dorsal cubiodenonavicular ligament

Dorsal cuneocubiod ligament

Dorsal cuneonavicular ligaments

Dorsal intercuneiform ligaments

View: Dorsal

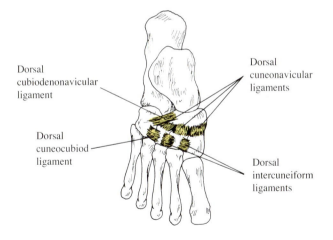

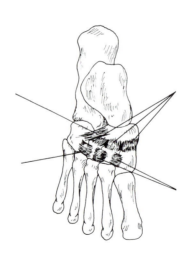

Intertarsal Joints
(Cuneonavicular, Cubideonavicular, Intercuneiform, and Cuneocuboid Joints)

Innervation: Branches of the deep peroneal and medial and lateral plantar nerves.

Arteries: Branches of the dorsalis pedis and medial and lateral plantar arteries.

Movements: Slight gliding and rotation at these joints contributes to inversion and eversion of the foot.

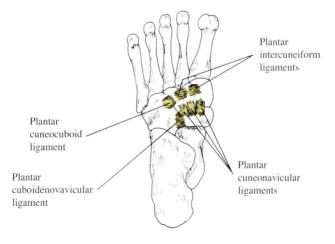

Plantar intercuneiform ligaments

Plantar cuneocuboid ligament

Plantar cuboidenovavicular ligament

Plantar cuneonavicular ligaments

View: Plantar

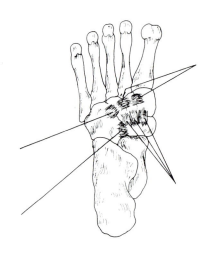

Tarsometatarsal and Intermetatarsal Joints

Innervation: Branches of the deep peroneal and medial and lateral plantar nerves.

Arteries: Plantar arch and arcuate branch of the dorsalis pedis artery.

Movements: Slight gliding during inversion and eversion of the foot.

View: Dorsal   *View: Plantar*

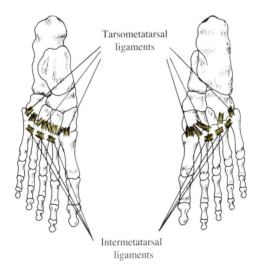

Tarsometatarsal
ligaments

Intermetatarsal
ligaments

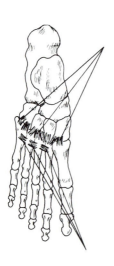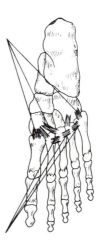

Metatarsophalangeal and Intermetatarsal Joints

Innervation: Plantar digital branches of medial plantar (medial 3 1/2 toes) and lateral plantar (lateral 1 1/2 toes) nerves.

Arteries: Plantar digital branches of the plantar arch and dorsal digital branches of arcuate branch of the dorsalis pedis artery.

Movements: Metatarsophalangeal joint: Flexion - extension, abduction - adduction. Interphalangeal joint: Flexion - extension.

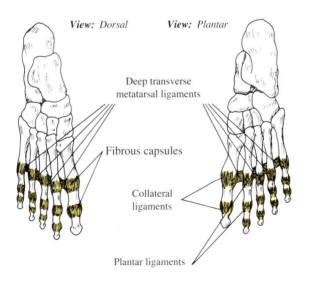

View: Dorsal   *View: Plantar*

Deep transverse metatarsal ligaments

Fibrous capsules

Collateral ligaments

Plantar ligaments

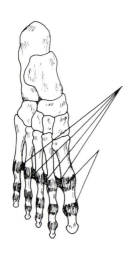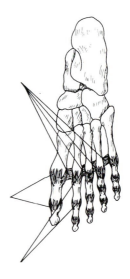

Terminology

SUPERIOR:
(Cranial)   Toward the head; toward the upper part of the structure.

INFERIOR:
(Caudal)   Away from the head; toward the lower part of the structure.

ANTERIOR:
(Ventral)   Nearer to or at the front of the body.

POSTERIOR:
(Dorsal)   Nearer to or at the back of the body, or the top of the foot.

MEDIAL: Nearer the midline of the body.

LATERAL: Farther from the midline of the body.

PROXIMAL: Nearer the attachement of a limb to the trunk.

DISTAL: Away from the attachment of a limb to the trunk.

EXTERNAL:
(Superficial)   Toward the surface of the body.

INTERNAL:
(Deep)   Away from the surface of the body.

PLANTAR: The sole or towards the sole of the foot.

Movement In Joints

Abduction: Movement away from axis of trunk, as in raising arms to the side horizontally, leg sideways and scapula away from the spinal column.

Adduction: Movement toward axis of trunk, as in lowering arms to the side or leg back to position.

Circumduction: Circular movement of joint, combining movements; possible in shoulder joint, hip joint and the trunk around a fixed point.

Dorsiflexion: Movement of top of foot toward anterior tibia bone.

Eversion: Turning sole of foot outward; weight on inner edge of the foot.

Extension: Straightening; moving bones apart as in the elbow joint when hand moves away from shoulder; exception shoulder and hip joints - a return movement of the humerus or femur downward, is considered extension.

Flexion: Bending: bringing bones together as in the elbow when hand is drawn to shoulder; exception shoulder and hip joints - movement of the humerus or femur to the front, upward is considered flexion.

Inversion: Turning sole of foot inward, weight on outer edge of the foot.

Plantar flexion: Movement of sole of foot downward toward the floor.

Pronation: Rotation on axis of bone, specifically applied to forearms, as in turning hand down by rotating radius on the ulna.

Internal rotation or medial rotation: Rotation with axis of bone toward the body, as when humerus is turned inward.

External rotation or lateral rotation: Rotation with axis of bone away from the body, as when the humerus is turned outward.

Supination: Rotation on axis of bone, specifically applied to forearms, as in turning hand up by rotating the radius on the ulna.

Published by Bryan Edwards Publishing Company
Produced by Bryan E. Nash
Written and Illustrated by Flash Anatomy, Inc.
Anatomical Illustrations by Meredith Albertelli
Graphics by Bianca M. Montoya

Thanks to Randolph E. Perkins PhD.,
Assistant Professor of Physical Therapy and Anatomy at
Northwestern University Medical School, for his contribution
and advice.